Lost Dutchman Mine Discoveries

And a History of Arizona Mining

By

Jay Fraser

Affiliated Writers of America / Publishers
Tempe, Arizona

Printed in the United States of America
by Ben Franklin Press / Tempe

Copyright © 1988 by Jay Fraser
Published by
Affiliated Writers of America
P.O. Box 2006
Tempe, Arizona 85281

Library of Congress 88-71430
ISBN 0918080576
1st Printing   1988
2nd Printing   1989

All rights reserved, including the right to reproduce this book or portions thereof without written permission from the publisher. All inquiries should be addressed to Affiliated Writers of America.

Cover Design and Art by Randy Galloway

Pen Dot Drawing of the Dutchman by Kelley Sands
(Back Cover and also on Page 54)

Map of Dutchman's Landmarks by Gary Kuhstoss

Color Photography by Jay Fraser
Cover Photo: The Rock in the Shape of a Man's Head

Color Separations by Tru Colour, Inc., Phoenix, Arizona

Dedicated to

Bernadine, Lorri and Mandy

CONTENTS

	Illustrations	v
	Foreword	vi
1	Mines, Maps, and Trails	1
2	Spaniards, Indians and Centuries of Stories	12
3	The End of Spanish Control	41
4	The End of Mexican Control	47
5	The Man in the Shadows: 1848 to 1862	55
6	Claims	67
7	The Military Trail and Weaver's Needle	85
8	The Dutchman's Trail	107
9	The Lands Between Carefree and Horseshoe Lake	111
	Map of Dutchman's Landmarks	116
	Author's Note	118
	Acknowledgements	120

ILLUSTRATIONS

Plate 1: Old Spanish Arrastra	10
Plate 2: Stone Tablet - Heart (Not Inserted)	11
Plate 3: Stone Tablet - Heart (Inserted)	14
Plate 4: Circle of Rocks Ruins Near Carefree	15
Plate 5: Stone Tablet - The Horse of the Santa Fe	18
Plate 6: Stone Tablet - Priest with Cross	19
Plate 7: Stone Tablet - Map	22
Plate 8: Blue Mountain	23
Pen Dot Drawing of the Dutchman by Kelley Sands	54
Plate 9: Rock in the Shape of a Man's Head	89
Plate 10: Stone Tablet - Cross	92
Plate 11: Horse Rock (Man on the Horse)	93
Plate 12: The Eye of the Needle	96
Plate 13: Black Top Mesa	97
Plate 14: Needle Rock at Verde River	100
Plate 15: Sombrero Butte	101
Plate 16: Sombrero Mountain	104
Map of Dutchman's Landmarks	116

FOREWORD

On the subject of the Lost Dutchman mine, one can practically believe anything he or she wants. Because it's probably been said already. Everything from the discovery of the mine itself to the certainty that it never existed appears in print, somewhere.

The location of the Lost Dutchman Mine has eluded the efforts of adventurers for over a hundred years and to some, that has meant that it never existed. To others, it has made it all the more important. For some, it has meant a tragic ending. But the story has survived, ironically encrusted in Jacob Waltz's own words: "No miner will ever find my mine."

Now there's an opportunity to see something new. To think something new which is based on the discovery of landmarks so visually powerful that their evidence cannot be ignored. The way they fit together into the Dutchman's story is equally powerful. Like many of the best riddles, once you know the answer, they're easy. But until you know, they're impossible. The Dutchman's riddle that no miner would ever find his mine is just such a riddle.

The twist is that the Dutchman referred to his mine as "an old Spanish working." Thus, the discovery of the Lost Dutchman Mine is also a clue to the maps of old Spanish mines. The question of, "What is left to be discovered in

Arizona?" is of central importance. Regarding the early exploration and mining of Arizona, it is apparent that references to the location of many specific sites--mountains, villages, and even rivers--is unclear. From the time of Coronado through the time of the Dutchman, there has been much speculation regarding which peak, which village, which river men have referred to in the record of their words. Correspondingly, Arizona is probably one of the richest states in the country regarding opportunity for discovery.

How this all relates to the present is matter of the diligence of minds and feet. And to discover something in the desert, it does mean walking. You won't see it from the car window, even from the Jeep window. Because it's been hidden and covered up, both by the men and the elements of a hundred years.

The overwhelming body of writing on this subject revolves around the search for the Lost Dutchman Mine near Apache Junction. But comparing the evidence, it is the overwhelming belief of this author that this will change.

Jay Fraser
March 1988

Chapter 1

Mines, Maps, and Trails

The story of mining in Arizona is a treacherous one, and the most treacherous of them all--the story of the Lost Dutchman Mine. Most of the stories about the Lost Dutchman Mine are stories about men who searched for it, many of whom lost their lives in some mysterious manner in the desert region of the Superstition Mountains. Other stories are based upon maps allegedly showing how to find the mine. Maps which have been sold and some of which have led men to their deaths. Ironically, true copies of any such maps are rare, and published references to such maps often refer to "facsimiles" rather than "authentic reproductions." Why aren't the true maps available in the literature?

Still other stories are about the people who knew the Dutchman, Jacob Waltz. Those who knew Jake claimed to also know certain things about the mine, and some of them spent many years searching for the gold and famous stash. There have been many accusations regarding the integrity of those who knew Jake, allegations of misdoings at Jake's hour of death, and many other questions remain unanswered regarding the nature of occurrences and utterances since Jake died in severe illness. There have been many references to this information in the telling of the story of the mine, as well as efforts to locate the mine.

Then there are the stories about the Superstition Mountains which are also "about" the Lost Dutchman Mine, and also "about" other mines in the area. Heavy with interpretation and extrapolation of various maps and Jake's "voice," the Superstition Mountains have become synonymous with the Lost Dutchman Mine. Weaver's Needle has been so closely tied to the mine's "true" location that massive search efforts have revolved around the immediate proximity of that landmark. And practically everything from Apache Junction to Canyon Lake is either named after the famous mine, or soon will be.

There are also stories about the Dutchman himself, Jacob Waltz. Murder, treachery, high grading and poverty seem to be the general scenario with Jake hiding out and covering his tracks. Apache Indian fights, the death (or murder) of his partner, and the stories of pure gold the Dutchman brought to town are mixed with stories of a quiet, reclusive life in Phoenix where the Dutchman was known to hold property and dwell. The contrast creates confusion. There's pure gold on one hand, and poverty on the other. Many questions arise, such as, why didn't he file a claim?

Still other stories are about mining in general in the Arizona area. There have been numerous accounts of discoveries and mining developments which stretch back to the time of the earliest Spanish exploration of what is presently Arizona. Rich with accounts of gold, but still richer in accounts of folly, the story of mining carries tremendous intrigue. Why? Because it is quite possible, and likely, that the richest gold mines in Arizona remain virtually untouched--remain to be discovered--maybe for the second--or third or fourth time. By comparing the stories of famous lost mines, many details seem to overlap. Many references coincide, descriptions of landmarks appear over and over again, and stories which seemingly have no correlation begin to bear striking resemblance to each other. Why? Because the stories may have one thing in common. They might be about the same places.

Among the tales and legends are people and places. The stories themselves are timeless. The value of the mines is priceless. A very important element in understanding "lost mines" is time. A perspective based on the date of exploration and discovery will yield an understanding which is much different than language lacking the color of time. One must recognize those things which change with time, particularly those aspects pertaining to civilized man's ethics and morals. One must also recognize those things which never change. This conglomerate of time and peoples, of landscape and exploration, of discovery and correlating events, of change and solidarity can actually make sense. Stories align, patterns repeat, and understanding emerges from tales which to some have no basis in reality, but which to others are the fire of their imagination, and yet to others become so real that they hold the crusted ore in their own hands.

A walk through the desert brings a sense of timelessness, a sense of solidarity in a land which repels the very footsteps of man. A land so rugged that horses are replaced by mules, a land so rugged that a rattlesnake can easily be encroached upon and coiled in defense. A land where cactus seems to jump out and grab even the most wary and cautious. Exploration of this land is among the most dangerous in North America, even in the 1980's. Imagine a hundred years ago. Imagine two hundred years to three hundred years ago. Explorers in a hostile land where virtually nothing was known.

So now, in the 1980's, the consensus is that everything worth finding has been found. That everything lost is lost for good, or never existed. These are faint hearted strokes against man, strokes from a brush wide enough to push the masses into a paint can and close the lid. *Last Sunday we explored an area which according to the stone tablet, had eight Peralta mines. We drove in with four wheel drive and parked several miles in. It was summer and getting hot quick even though it was seven in the morning when we parked. How could you wait for fall? We went in through the old road, boulders and rocks and gullies where the stream ran fifteen feet deep in a heavy rain. The way was steep and the water could rip away anything when it ran. The mountains were hills and the hills were mountains, how could you know which was which, they were so big and there were so many and we wound through them with brush and thicket trees so dense that you couldn't see five feet. Five feet, mind you, not five hundred yards, five feet!*

And yet, we looked, we scoured with our eyes, we knew. The sun moved up a little in the sky and it got hot and we walked a steady pace with an eye for rattlers and about a mile in, there! Look there! And my eyes followed an old mule trail on the side of the hill, I could see where it had been constructed in the rocky brush, little stacks of rock held up the precarious edges where the hill was too steep to hold a cut trail, where the dirt would fall out of the bottom of the cut and take a mule down, tightly fitted rock, packed into a little wall, a little stand that had held over a hundred years. And the trail, my eyes followed it down where it wound into the stream bed where it widened and had trees and bushes and in a tiny gap, through a tiny break in the green leaves, was an old arrastra (Plate 1, page 10). Yes, yes, just as on the map. We slid down the steep bank, our Vibram soles biting and tearing into the dirt and the brush tearing into our shirt sleeves and baggy pants, and we crossed the dry stream bed and stepped up to the old working area. The trails came in from two directions and the arrastra was intact. The Peraltas had processed their ore here, and how much ore? Well, you could see rock after rock, worn out. There were five rocks that I could identify in my 1987 treck. This was a big one; they had cut a live tree down and left a two foot stump which they drove an iron peg into. They built a trough around the stump, and the mules would drag a large stone through the trough to mash the ore, to crush the gold out. The rock trough was still tight, it could still be used. The rocks were worn smooth as silk. I brushed my hand over one of the rocks which they had dragged through the trough. I put my finger into the hole they bored in the rock to drag it. They must have driven a wooden peg into that hole to attach the chain. And these drag rocks were worn out, used so long that they wore down and were discarded as they became too light. Now they processed all this ore, and, the mule trails, they would lead to the mines themselves. Eight of them, according to the map. We'd found the arrastra, and we went on up for the mines.

The maps are real, the stories are real, and the mines are real. The fact is, the desert terrain is so rugged that you could literally walk over an old mine and not know it. They were hidden, they have been filled in, covered, vegetated and washed clear by years of rain. You wouldn't know, without the map. You wouldn't know, without the story. And who hid them? Who buried these old mines? People who with their own motives, with their own reasons why, wouldn't have you discover a gold mine. And who buries the stories? Another question is, how does one bury a story? By telling something different, maybe. By lying, maybe. Or maybe, and most probably, by assuming the wrong meaning. An interpretation of a landmark, for example, can send someone forty miles up the wrong river! Now how would you find a mine which you could step on and not see, if you went forty miles up the wrong river? There's a lot of laughing going on, the laughter of a hundred years, howling at the heels of anyone who takes lost mine stories seriously, but those who laugh loudest are those who know, in their heart, that the mines exist. They might even be experts on the subject who hold the true maps, and sell the facsimiles.

Now why would they do that? Would that be fair, sending people out, to plod along, to risk their lives, maybe just to have a good ole trail ride and look for landmarks which, if only they could find, would lead them where? Where? Follow that two dollar map? The one with Weaver's Needle? Well, everybody knows where Weaver's Needle is, but what about the Eye of the Needle? What about Sombrero Butte? What about Sombrero Mountain? The Rock Horse? If someone found all those, then they'd have the key to some of the maps which circulate like so many napkins at the bar. But if someone had the real map, it would be great if other people would search for the keys, search for the landmarks which would unlock the mystery of the map. Yes, the holder of the true map could sit back and prime the prospectors, waiting for the real landmarks to be discovered so they could go and find the lost mines.

But maybe some of these maps floating around are real. Yes, in fact, they are. Some of them have been cut into stone and don't "float" around so easily, and some are in the Mesa Southwest Museum where everyone can come and see for themselves. Where everyone can come in and pan for gold in the little stream they built there, and imagine they are the Dutchman himself, panning for gold in Arizona, and look at the stone tablets carefully locked behind glass walls. Yes, just like the Dutchman. More than they know. As much as they could dream, it's true. Because those stone tablets are real, and nearly all of the landmarks have been identified. A large number of lost Spanish mines can now be rediscovered in the area east and north of Carefree.

I was talking with a forest ranger one day and told him I was writing a book which would reveal the location of landmarks pertaining to lost mine maps. When I informed him of the number of mines which could now be rediscovered, he said to me, "Then why would you publish it?" I smiled, because, among other things, it raised the question of "what's important in life?" Now, to think about all the men, all the lives, their dreams, their imaginations, their discoveries, their follies, and even their deaths. Hundreds of years, thousands of men, searching, dreaming, searching, dreaming, searching, dreaming, telling! These things may not be important to some men, but they are the essence of life to others. It is the latter group to whom this book will have meaning, and the first group will have a chance to understand.

So now, go to the Mesa Southwest Museum and see for yourself, see these stone tablets, imagine for yourself, and then follow your heart. Because even the map tells you that (in Spanish): "Study the heart. I go eighteen places" (Plate 6, page 19). Now keep in mind, eighteen places doesn't mean eighteen mines, because some of the "places" show eighteen mines. Some show eight, or seven. Multiply these numbers by eighteen. In all, probably a hundred and fifty mines remain to be discovered from these stone tablets. But of all the meanings in the maps, there is one statement which no one would question in truth: "This trail is dangerous."

Plate 1: Old Spanish Arrastra - Still Intact Off Seven Springs Road

Plate 2: Stone Tablet (Without Stone Heart Inserted) (Mesa Southwest Museum)

Chapter 2

Spaniards, Indians, and Centuries of Stories

Gold in Arizona took the dimensions of magnitude in or near the year 1539 when Fray Marcos de Niza had a story so incredible that he could not even tell Coronado, but had to speak directly to the viceroy himself. Coronado and de Niza went to Mexico City together to visit Viceroy Mendoza. There is considerable debate over what transpired in the way of conversations but the result was another expedition northward. It was arranged in much the same way that de Niza first went into the Arizona area: as quietly as possible. The idea of seven cities paved with gold had been circulating in Spain since before the year 1200.

There was a great drought which lasted some twenty years in the late 1200's in the Arizona area. The Anasazi Indians apparently moved down from the Verde River area and the upper Salt River area during this time, settling into the Gila River area, and that area around Casa Grande. This would have been the time of abandonment of the Montezuma's Castle area north of Phoenix. These people were also known as the Salado Indians, since they came from the Rio Salado/Salt River area (Plate 4, page 15). These Indians merged with the Hohokams and built the Big House in Casa Grande. There are numerous mysteries surrounding the construction of the Big House, such as the sun holes in the walls. Light passes through both holes only on March 6 and 7, and again on October 6 and 7. The dates are respectively, two weeks before spring equinox, and two weeks after fall equinox. There are other sets of holes which are not yet understood. There is also an unsolved labyrinthine design on an interior wall. These Indians were originally of a cliff dwelling pueblo type. They had lived in the area of some very rich gold deposits, and since they had demonstrated considerable architectural talent (some of which escapes our understanding), did they in fact construct what might have been known to the Hohokams and other southern Indians as some "great cities to the north"? The probability of de Niza telling the truth is in his favor when these things are considered.

The question is, what did de Niza really see? Many believe that he lied and saw nothing. But one of the things that hasn't changed about men through the ages is their reluctance to tell the details of their discoveries of gold.

Plate 3: Stone Tablet (With Stone Heart Inserted) Mesa Southwest Museum Circle of Rocks Ruins Appears on Tablet as " ◉ "

Plate 4: Circle of Rocks Ruins Near Carefree
(Where Mateo Manje Probably Stood According to Diary)

Marcos de Niza refused to speak to anyone about what he'd discovered, including Coronado, and would only speak directly to the viceroy himself. Whether de Niza "knew" there was gold in Arizona, or simply "thought" there was gold in Arizona is something difficult to know. But the result of what he told Viceroy Mendoza was an expedition to find gold. The fact is, there have been several very rich gold mines found and operated in Arizona, so there is no question that the gold was (is) in Arizona. And it is also known that the Anasazis lived in the same area as the rich gold mines. There are the present remains of Montezuma's Castle and Tuzigoot, both along the Verde River and now National Monuments. Both were occupied about the year 1200. And then there is the Tonto National Monument at the junction of Tonto Creek and the Salt River. These consisted of three- to five-story structures, with as many as seventy-five rooms. There are also mines in Sonora, Mexico. Fray Marcos de Niza in all probability did see gold in Arizona, heard about the great cities to the north, and told Viceroy Mendoza about it. It could have been rich outcroppings, it could have been nuggets in streams or rivers. And it is well known that some Arizona "free gold" is so pure that it doesn't have to be smelted. There seems little basis to doubt the integrity of de Niza.

Next? A story about gold in the Superstitions would naturally spark into a fire about The Dutchman Mine. And similarly, a story about gold from de Niza's travels would spark into a fire about the "seven cities paved with gold." The next thing you know it's diamond studded arrowheads. You can bet that Coronado's men were immeasurably enthusiastic as they went northward into what we now call Arizona. The real trouble with de Niza's story is the cities of gold, not the idea of gold itself, nor the idea of cities. At the time of this writing, there seems to be no evidence of any Indian or aboriginal civilization in Arizona which practiced gold metallurgy, although it is believed that the Hohokams practiced copper metallurgy and produced at least some copper bells. Therefore, the cities of gold seem absurd. This has been taken to mean that because no gold evidence has been discovered, other than the stories, the cities never existed. It is not conclusive because there are other possibilities. Such as, we simply haven't found the evidence, i.e. the gold. Probably, the cities of gold never existed. Possibly, they did, and were dismantled when an army came looking. Indians have been known to do such things so well that it escapes the understanding of the Western World. Indians have also been known "not to tell" so well that it also escapes Western understanding. The role of Indians in the stories of gold in Arizona is one of distinct character and was probably a significant factor in the failure of Coronado and de Niza to find what they sought.

There is also another significant factor. Unless directly on the bank of a river such as the Gila or the Salt, it would have been nearly impossible for the de Niza party to find the

Plate 5: Stone Tablet - The Horse of the Santa Fe
(Mesa Southwest Museum)

Plate 6: Stone Tablet - Priest with Cross
(Mesa Southwest Museum)

same spot again in Arizona. In present day Arizona, it's tough, even going into the same twenty square mile area. In 1540, we're talking of a vast area of the entire state, and then some. When historians question whether de Niza actually saw the Gulf of California from Sonora, then why can't they see that compared to the Gulf, a gold outcropping is infinitely small? Maybe de Niza simply couldn't find it again. Speculation could, and will, go on until new evidence comes to the surface. But as a beginning, the story of gold started here, and grew in much the same way, some three hundred years later.

What's most important of all, at this point, is how the Peraltas got started mining in Arizona. This Mexican family from Sonora, Mexico, worked mines in Arizona prior to the 1840's when it was part of the Spanish Territory. When did they explore? And how did they keep it so quiet, when it is known that they had some four hundred peons working mines near and in the Superstitions?

With regard to the years between the 1540's and the 1640's, mining accounts are vague, but things have a way of slipping out. One such account is given by a deserter of the Spanish army, whose written words prior to his execution survived as a result of church records. It was a slip. Significant mining activity is indicated in the account of Pedro Navarez, a Mexican peon who had become a soldier in the Spanish army. He had accompained the Spanish on many of their expeditions and undertakings to the north, and apparently as far north as Santa Fe, New Mexico. Pedro Navarez deserted the Spanish army in 1639, apparently because of abuses by superiors, and befriended the Apaches. It is said that for ten years Pedro lived with the Apaches and learned their ways. He is also said to have accompanied them on their raids upon Spanish pack trains which transported gold and silver back to Mexico.

Pedro was captured by the Spanish in 1649 and returned to Mexico for trial, where he was convicted of treason and sentenced to death. Pedro made a confession in writing for the absolution of his soul before his hanging in that same year, and many years later his confession surfaced in the midst of other church records. It included a waybill which described the whereabouts of tremendous amounts of gold and silver. Among the descriptions are the references to a large stone with a cross, a small plot of ground a hundred yards below, a small stone, and 18 "atajos." The word "atajo" means cross-path or by-path. Some have interpreted this information to correlate to the area of the Coballo Mountains near Santa Fe, New Mexico, but there is an interesting twist: the description bears remarkable resemblance to the drawings and descriptions on the stone tablets on display in the Mesa Southwest Museum, apparently found near the Superstition Mountains in Arizona in 1949. On the tablet which reads "EL COBOLLO DE SANTA FE" there also appears the name "PEDRO" (Plate 5, page 18). On the tablet with the figure of the saint, the

Plate 7: Stone Tablet (Mesa Southwest Museum)

Plate 8: Blue Mountain

saint is holding a cross. Beneath the cross there is the small heart-shaped figure which could be the small stone Pedro was referring to. So Pedro described 18 "atajos," and one stone tablet says "YO BOY 18 LUGARES" which translates into "I go 18 places" (lugar means "place, spot, village"). At the extreme right edge of one of the tablets are the words "SONORA MEX" (Plate 6, page 19).

The account of Pedro Navarez bears striking resemblance to the stone tablets apparently carved in either 1747 or 1847 (Plate 2, page 11), some one- to two-hundred years later, and this is a strong indication that there was a continued mining effort by the Spanish through the 1600's. It is also a strong indication that knowledge of the location of these mines was passed on through the next two hundred years, that somewhere else the knowledge existed. Very quietly.

The gap up to the 1840's narrows somewhat further with the accomplishments of Father Kino, from the 1640's to the 1680's. Reinforcing the strength of the Anasazis at Big House, the Jesuit priest Kino described it as "casa grande--a four-story building as large as a castle and equal to the finest church in these lands of Sonora."

But with regard to Father Kino and his exploration, it is the words from the diary of a fellow traveler by the name of Captain Mateo Manje which reveals knowledge at the time of a story of innumerable gold and silver mines in an area near Blue Mountain and the Verde River. The entry is dated

March 2, 1699 and is in reference to a guided trip which Father Kino, Mateo Manje, and their "guides" took into the area.

"Traveling east and climbing to the top of a small mountain, which the guides pointed out to us, we could see plainly the Verde River, which takes its rise in the land of the Apaches, running northeast to southeast, with a grove of trees along its banks. It is joined by another, salty river, running from east to west, and the two merging together flow into this Rio Grande, the junction of which we were able to see."

"[the Verde River] flows by a mountain streaked with several veins of green, blue and variegated colored stones. We do not know if this could be the Blue Mountain of which a tale is told, to the effect that innumerable gold and silver mines, very rich and of high grade ore, have been discovered. The conquerors of New Mexico [which included Arizona at the time], at the time when they came to this place, took some ore to be refined; but they never returned. As the years passed, only the tradition of the Blue Mountain remained."

The Verde River referred to here is believed to be the same Verde River of today, and the "salty river" was the Salt River of today. The "Rio Grande" is not referred to as "The Rio Grande" but as "<u>this</u> Rio Grande" and is probably a reference to the Salt River below the junction of the Salt and Verde. The writer may not have known how else to refer to the combined rivers. This could also be a reference to the Gila, as Rio Grande was one of the former names given to the Gila and the Salt and Verde do empty into the Gila.

Now what's important here is, first, who were the guides? Indians? Or other Spaniards familiar with the area, more familiar than Father Kino. Second, there is the reference to the small mountain from which they could see the concourse of the Verde and Salt. Third, there is the reference to Blue Mountain. Is it the same mountain as the presently named Blue Mountain (Plate 8, page 23) in the vicinity of the concourse of the Verde and Salt? And fourth, there is reference to very rich, high grade ore in gold and silver mines in the area. Putting these references together in terms of landmarks, we have the concourse of the Verde and Salt, the Blue Mountain, a rich area of innumerable gold and silver mines, and the top of a small mountain from which the concourse of the two rivers is visible.

The area Mateo Manje refers to is obviously that area of land near the Verde River which is just below Bartlett Lake, near Blue Mountain. It is probable that the top of the small mountain he refers to as having stood upon is the small mountain just off Seven Springs Road which is well known for its Circle of Rocks at the very top (Plate 4, page 15). Just below the Circle of Rocks is the Rock in the Shape of a Man's Head (Plate 9, page 89). From this point, the view is as Mateo Manje describes, and it is one of the few points in the area from which you can see the concourse of the Verde and Salt. The canyons directly below this hill connect with Rackensack Canyon and Camp Creek, which provides access to both the Verde River and Blue Mountain. The most probable route that they took to the Circle of Rocks would have been to cross the Salt River somewhere near the present location of Tempe, proceed north along the old Pima Trail which is now called Pima Road, and then east from some point near the present town of Carefree, to the small mountaintop where many, many Indian artifacts have been found. The area to the east is also described as the land of the Apaches, and that may have had bearing upon their route. The Apaches are known to have lived along the Verde, and it is claimed in the text that innumerable mines had been discovered in the area. It is also claimed that the conquerors, and first discoverers, never returned. Why not? Rich, high grade ore is mentioned, but no reason for abandonment. Mateo Manje, having made the connection between the Blue Mountain he saw and the Blue Mountain in the story, may have enabled the Jesuits to follow up on the story and find the mines in the area. It is also possible that these mines had been worked all along, secretly, without Manje's knowledge. But what did the "guides" of Father Kino and Mateo Manje know about these mines?

Obviously, there was knowledge and belief of significant discoveries in the area. But the area near Blue

Mountain and up Camp Creek from the Verde River has hardly been explored, even today. And now there is strong evidence that the Horse of the Santa Fe stone tablet in the Mesa Southwest Museum describes the area of Blue Mountain and Camp Creek, just below Bartlett Dam Road. People have been looking in the wrong area, in the middle of the Superstitions for all these lost mines. When potent exploration gets rolling in this Blue Mountain area, people are going to find the old workings. People are going to find mining artifacts which will clarify the dates and extent of mining by the Spaniards, Jesuits and Mexicans in the area. The discovery of the landmarks which identify the area is only the beginning. The best discoveries are yet to be made.

I came across a couple of stories in a book titled <u>A Motif Index</u> *by Byrd Howell Granger and read about the Lost Treasure of Montezuma Head. Montezuma Head is described as a rock formation in the Estrella Mountains and northwest of Redrock. Recent discoveries of landmarks, however, indicate that it is located near the Verde River in the same area as the early Anasazi settlements, which is also a rich gold area, which is also north of Three Red Hills. Blue Mountain is not only in the same area, Blue Mountain is one of the Three Red Hills, and is red when viewed from one particular angle. From other angles, the blue rock of Blue Mountain stands out.*

According to an account from an old Indian chief to his

son, one of the first Spanish priests coming to Arizona deserted and settled on the Gila River where he mined gold with the help of Indians. Under pressure from Apaches on the warpath, the former priest packed out the gold with the help of sixty Indians and transported it to the Head where it was buried in a cave under the chin of the Head. The priest is said to have sealed the Indians in the cave along with the gold. The Indian chief whose son told the story used to bring down gold from the mountains but other Indians refused to go near because they believed it was haunted.

From the cities founded in Sonora to San Xavier del Bac near present day Tucson, we move forward into the 1700's. A map dated 1701 shows the Jesuit missions and visitas. The symbolic indication for each mission on the map revealed whether they were "blessed" or not blessed. Missions not blessed were referred to as visitas. A visita was a church of sorts but one which is periodically visited by a priest rather than occupied by a permanant priest in charge. Visitas were also for purposes other than religion, and in all, Father Kino founded twenty-nine missions and seventy-three visitas. One such visita appears unblessed on the banks of the Gila River. This is probably the "weigh station" where the Jesuit gold was brought and processed for shipping to Mexico City and then by ship to Spain.

Many Spanish galleons laden with gold never made it to Spain as a result of either pirates or storms, and it's possible that this contributed to the distrust of the Jesuits in not paying taxes. It has been claimed that Father Kino never finished one of the bell towers at San Xavier Mission in order to avoid taxes, because an unfinished mission could not be taxed until completed. Other tax evasions may have taken place, including individual priest corruption and greed. Sentiments against the Jesuits grew astronomically in the 1740's as reports of huge silver and gold stashes found their way back to royalty in Spain. Several mines were ordered closed, and the Franciscans were eager to take control over the Jesuit domain. In any event, the Jesuits lost control over their mining operations and were expelled from the territory between 1747 and 1769 (depending upon which historical account to consider as accurate) for hoarding gold and not paying their one-fifth portion of mined gold to the King of Spain. They were banished from the lands for a period of one hundred years.

The stone tablets at the Mesa Museum may have been carved by the Jesuits in the year 1747, and dated 1847 to indicated the date of the planned return of the Jesuits. It is also possible that the Jesuits, hearing of their possible banishment, smuggled their church gold to the "weigh station" to be melted down and hidden in a great cache for future generations. Thus, they would have used the trails and men who previously carried gold to Mexico City, for the reverse transport of gold to the territory north of San Xavier, to the terrritory of the "weigh station."

The Jesuits were removed and other Spaniards came,

and they established primarily military settlements, but the settlement and mission building process in Arizona was constantly one of "hanging on" rather than growth and expansion. This is largely attributable to the efforts of the Indians, most notably the Apaches, and also to the hostility of the land.

There were the continuous pack trains which supplied the missions in the southern Arizona area, so there was some travel, although the fact that the Apaches managed to totally sack even the stronghold of San Xavier del Bac in 1767 gives some perspective on the risk of exploration. The entire effort of the Spanish collapsed near that time and their advances north of San Xavier usually resulted in heavy losses from Apache attacks. It is interesting to note that many of the Jesuits were Germans and that numerous stories of "their" gold discoveries and lost treasures are still in circulation, and naturally, often related to the Lost Dutchman Mine.

Geronimo claimed that the Apaches had found a gold mine and that the Spaniards seized the mine. The seizure was said to have occurred in 1767 and Spanish soldiers are thought to have remained approximately one year to work the mine. The Indians fought them constantly and eventually killed all but two of the Spaniards. These survivors are said to have hidden the gold in the tunnel and escaped to Tubac. They never returned, but they are said to have left a map which showed an Indian profile cut by nature on a cliff. Geronimo is said to have told a friend that his mine was in the Verde River country and that there was an Indian head profile carved by nature on a high cliff above the mine opening. Also there was an arrastra built by the Spanish near a spring under a large boulder. There was fresh water in the three sided canyon and a rock slide is said to have covered much of the Spanish workings. The canyon is said to be so steep that the Spaniards had to lower themselves into it with the use of ropes. The Apaches are thought to have killed many of the Spaniards by rolling large rocks down upon them. Some say this mine is in Sycamore Canyon, but like many speculations about location, the landmarks had not been identified. The recent discovery of the Rock Head places the mine in the Camp Creek area above the Verde River.

Another account related to the Stone Head is that it was the Apache Thunder God. According to accounts based on Apache stories, gold and silver were given by the Apache Thunder God, and not to be taken. The area of the Thunder God was sacred ground. The land and caves beneath the Thunder God are said to be both the source of gold and silver, and the location of the spoils of Apache raids, including those of Geronimo.

There may be some link between the date of the Spanish seizure of the "Apache mine" and the sacking of San Xavier, both occuring in 1767. It could be that one or more Jesuits had worked the mine and had Indians doing the labor until the collapse of the entire Spanish effort, notably, in 1767. Spaniards moving into the area at that time may have attacked not only the Apaches but any Jesuits who had escaped banishment, and took over the mine. This may have enraged the Apaches and resulted in the sacking of San Xavier. The three events happening in the same year indicate a very strong possibility of some connection between the three.

There are many accounts of mining activity by the Spaniards between the years 1590 and 1767 and although any specific mine site references are vague, the role of the Indians seems consistent. The Indians were either persuaded or forced to work the mines. It doesn't take much, just a little, thought, to see why the relationship between the Indians and the Spaniards deteriorated. Nor does it take much thought to figure out why Indians would refuse to lead the Spaniards to the places where gold lay in plain sight on the ground. As the Indians got wiser to the ways of the new explorers, it is quite understandable that they would begin hiding gold outcroppings and any other gold they knew about. It is quite understandable that tribal members would be forbidden from even visiting the sites by their chiefs. Talk of gold from Indians probably vanished, and was replaced by a negative shake of the head. It is even possible that the Indians, in the same manner of regard for gold and the Spaniards, banished gold metallurgy and all traces of it from the land, and erased or hid any evidence that they came across. Such an activity, carried out for several hundred years, might be very thorough.

With regard to gold obtained between 1590 and 1767, the Spaniards were required to pay a portion of all gold obtained to the King of Spain, and in the case of the Jesuits, it was one fifth. The stories of Jesuit gold stashes and "lost mines" usually revolve around efforts to beat the king out of his fifth, and/or the church out of the rest. Men will be men, even holy men will sometimes be men, with all the trappings including greed, lying and all the other shortcomings of mankind. How often this actually happened is probably less well known than the number of times accusations emerged from Spain and Mexico. But it certainly could have happened more than once. Maybe it didn't happen at all, although that seems to defy a rational sense of probability. In any case, stories about Jesuit caches have survived the years and are linked with landmarks which appear in seemingly unrelated lost mine stories. The link between Jesuit gold and other lost mines is probably one of the most difficult links to establish, at least at this time. But that may change when future discoveries supply the link.

An exploration by Padre Garces up the Gila River from San Xavier is known to have occurred in 1771. He went north to the area of Casa Grande, and then later that year all the way to the Colorado River. Other explorations by the Spaniards are not so well documented although prospecting of the Salt and Verde Rivers seems likely. Why wouldn't they? Even today, gold can be panned out of both the Verde and the Salt. The Spaniards had clearly demonstrated their willingness to destroy culture and take gold throughout Mexico. Gold was deeply ingrained in the hierarchy of their society. And it was the gold seeker who went exploring. Also, since water is scarce in much of Arizona, early exploration would naturally follow the rivers. It must be remembered that since the Indians had apparently not practiced gold metallurgy, gold and gold outcroppings existed in natural form, with gold right out in plain sight on the ground. For this reason, exploration could have been very exciting.

Little or no link seems to have been established or even suggested in published works to connect early Spanish prospecting to the prospecting of the Peralta family from Sonora although it is logical that they would follow up on whatever information or maps that they had from previous Spanish prospecting and mining. The period between the late 1700's and early 1800's seems to get overlooked as emphasis shifts away from the Spaniards and Mexicans and toward the westward expansion of the United States. Spanish exploration shifted in emphasis toward California, the lower Colorado River and the Yuma Indian territory in the 1780's and encountered plenty of trouble there. Missions fell to the Yumas near the Colorado and also to the Apaches in central Arizona. Tucson survived as a walled city, and the missions of San Xavier and Tumacacori survived. But in general, the Apaches had won and maintained a constant reign of terror and attack. Spain finally lost its hold in the Mexican Revolution of 1821, and that is probably the beginning of a new kind of exploration, the beginning of the exploration by Mexicans into their lands in Arizona.

But there's a curious twist in the history of Arizona land: The Peralta Land Grant of 1748. Apparently, Don Miguel Peralta de Cordoba received title to approximately 3,750 square miles of land along the Gila River in the heart of Arizona as a reward for services to Ferdinand VI of Spain. His Majesty titled him the Baron of the Colorados and granted the land on December 20, 1748, notably supporting the year of the loss of Jesuit control as being 1747. The land was said to have been granted for services to the crown. This raises an interesting question. What services? Gold? Probably so. Don Miguel is also said to have received confirmation of the grant from Ferdinand VI's successor, Carlos III.

The Spanish Crown had ordered the Jesuits out of the new territories and had titled other men to work and control the mines. The whole matter of mining during this later time remained secretive, just like with the Jesuits.

The stone tablets on display at the Mesa Museum were either made by the Jesuits in or near the year 1747, or they were made by the Peraltas in or near the year 1847 (Plate 2, page 11). Ironically, both the Jesuits and Peraltas lost legal title to their mining domains through political decree, the Jesuits through the King of Spain and the Peraltas through the Mexican-American War and the Gadsden Purchase.

Regardless of who carved them, the stone tablets describe the same geographic area in which both the Jesuits and Peraltas operated mines. Whether the Jesuit-carved tablets showed the Peraltas where the mines were, or whether the Peraltas found the mines through other sources and then carved the tablets themselves has not been determined at this time. References to Don Miguel Peralta implied or inherent in the tablets themselves do not prove them to be Peralta produced because the Jesuits could have been referring to the new assignee of the mining interests. But one thing that seems odd for the Jesuits is the misspelling of words on the tablets, unless it was intentional to provide clues or mislead followers.

The issue of the Peraltas is a confusing one. Don Miguel Peralta apparently died in 1788 and the estate went to Don Miguel Peralta II, who lived until 1864. A different account has Don Miguel Peralta's death in the year 1824, but if this were the case he would have lived seventy seven years beyond the date of the grant, which would make him very young to receive such a grant unless he lived beyond the age of one hundred years. It is more likely that he died in 1788 as previously stated, and it is also likely that the date of the birth of Don Miguel Peralta II is fairly accurate, dated by some to be in 1781.

Thusly, Don Miguel Peralta II would have died at the age of eighty three in 1864, had he lived that long. He apparently had three sons: Pedro, Manuel and Ramon. It is said that the father and all three sons were involved in the prospecting and mining of the Rio Salado area and that of its tributaries.

In all probability, Spanish gold mining in Sonora and Arizona was carried out very secretively and managed by the Peralta family beginning with the land grant of 1748 and continuing through the Mexican Revolution, the Mexican-American War and the Gadsden Purchase. Exploration, prospecting and mining would have been conducted quietly and continuously, as had been done since the 1500's by the Jesuits and other Spaniards through New Mexico (which at that time included Arizona). As with all closely guarded secrets throughout the history of mankind, the whereabouts of gold has consistently ranked among the best kept, and wise for the keeper. For those who doubt this wisdom, a simple perusal of mining litigation in Arizona would correct this error. A good place to start is the Vulture Mine in Arizona. There is such a maze of filings, cross-filings and litigation that its discoverer was in constant battle. Then there are the murders, hijacks, thefts, bribes, blackmailings, swindles and frauds in the area which were the downstream effects of the mining operations and transportation of gold bullion. Operating quietly, the

Peraltas had apparently learned that they could avoid a lot of trouble.

It is known that gold and silver mines were operated in Sonora and the Peralta family is said to have operated some of them. Since Mexican land included Arizona at the time, it is expected that such a family would have to brave the Apaches and explore land to the north to prospect. It is also probable that they had information and stories from the earlier Spanish explorers and mines. It is also probable that these Sonora mining families either directly supplied the Spanish missions and explorers, or knew those who did. In which case the men who ran the supply pack trains could very easily have done some prospecting on their own, just remember the "guides" of Father Kino and Captain Mateo Manje up the Verde in 1699. Whatever the case, the earliest gold that came out of Arizona went down into Sonora on its route to Mexico City or Spain. Someone supplied the animals and food. Someone supplied the labor. And as is always the case with these "someones," someone must have talked about the quantity and origins of the gold. But very little has crept into the history books. It is believed that the Jesuits sent some $60 billion in gold to Spain by galleons, and Spanish shipwrecks have been found with the gold still aboard. What part of Mexico, or New Mexico this gold came from is less known. The trails of Sonora had seen, by 1820, nearly three hundred years of travelers to and from Arizona, including whatever gold was brought out. And yet, Sonora in the history of Mexican and Arizona gold mining is as quiet as the Sonoran desert itself.

On one of my trips into Mexico, I was driving on an old dirt road in Front Sonora which was not too far from Caborca Mission which was founded in 1693. It was a bad road and risky without four wheel drive and it was near the waters of the Gulf of California. I'd pulled several Mexican travelers out of mires in the sand as I went along the road and although my Spanish is not very good, we managed to talk as the rope was connected between the trucks. I've always enjoyed the Mexicans of Sonora. They are friendly, hard working, honest, humble and for the most part, very religous. As I continued along my way in the direction of Caborca, a Jeep approached me from the other direction. We slowed as we were about to pass each other, and then stopped to talk. I leaned my arm out my open window and the Jeep had no window. He was American. We talked about where we were headed and he asked me if I'd been to the gold mine. Gold mine? I asked. He proceeded to tell me how to get there and he was very friendly. He wasn't interested in the gold for himself nor was anyone in his party, but it was an interesting place to visit. He produced a piece of ore in his hand and passed it over to me. There was plenty of gold in it, all right. From the mine in Sonora, near Caborca.

Chapter 3

The End of Spanish Control

The Mexican Revolution of 1821 marked the end of Spanish control in Mexico and Arizona, and *must* have had a dramatic effect upon mining in the area. And the political turmoil of the early 1800's in Arizona between Spain, Mexico and the United States was paralleled by renegade Apache attacks upon anyone and everyone. No one could travel safely. To the white man, the only good Apache was a dead one. To the Apache, the only good white man was a dead one. Put that together with cholla cactus, rugged desert mountains, lack of water, and very few trails and you have a scenario of tremendous danger with people often shot on sight. And those who didn't shoot at all were those who often went down in history as fools. Dead-on-the-spot fools, of course. Massacres and ambushed wagons and families brutally slain. No sense recounting all of those stories here, but they are important because they reflect a way of life. The danger was incredible. And the danger to mine gold at the time? Far greater.

But for those experienced in the ways of the desert and Apache Indians, it could be done. It was done. The Peraltas survived both the Mexican Revolution and the Apaches. And they continued their mining just as they had in the past, quietly, secretively. They traveled through incredibly rough terrain like the Superstition Mountains where no one else could, or would even dare, to travel. They avoided contact with everyone. Their secrets were closely guarded and their mines constructed in such a way that they were hard to see, often the tunnels were built beneath large bushes and the arrastras were constructed in obscure places well concealed by natural terrain. Their trails were built half way up the sides of mountains and hills instead of along the top of ridges and through stream beds where they could be seen.

It was difficult to follow the old trail. We had come into the valley by coming up the dry stream bed and that had been easy walking. We picked up the old trail where, according to the map, it crossed the stream. We walked up onto the trail and followed it and it went part way up the side of the hill and then along through the tall scrub which was thick and it was so thick we couldn't have left the trail if we wanted to, it was so thick along the sides. No one could have possibly seen us as we moved further up and along the side of the hill for part of a mile and then the trail turned back down and then crossed the stream, and here it had water in it, and for a moment we were in the open but there the stream bed had a turn in it below us, and another one above us, so we couldn't see very far in any direction. Once again, someone would have to be right up on us to see us or to see the trail. And moving on the trail as we did, it was impossible to tell where it would lead without the map because there were so many turns, up and down, across, and most often through some thick brush or rock, or at least hidden by the natural contours of the land.

The Peralta prospecting of the Salt and Verde River areas was probably completed long before "white men" ever came to Arizona as part of the exploration of the "West." The first record of an "American" to explore Arizona is that of James Ohio Pattie, his father, Sylvester, and their party of trappers. Apparently they had obtained a license to trap in Arizona from a Mexican official in New Mexico and came as far as Casa Grande. In 1832 Pauline Weaver made way, also, to Casa Grande where he carved his name into a wall as "P. Weaver 1832." But few, if any, other Americans came into Arizona prior to 1846. For one thing, they would have been entering Mexican land.

The Peraltas not only continued their mining and prospecting after the Mexican Revolution, they kept their land grant alive. The President of the new Mexican Republic, Antonio Lopez de Santa Anna, acknowledged the

Peralta Land Grant and executed a title to that effect which guaranteed its validity and propriety. But the fate of the Peralta Land Grant was similar to the fate of the Peralta mines.

The number of gold mines the Peraltas developed in Arizona during the early 1800's and prior to the Mexican American War is estimated to number in the hundreds. There is no known record of how much gold was transported back to Mexico during this time, just as there is no known record of the amount of gold taken out by the Spaniards during the previous three hundred years. Some cynics would assume that because there are no records, there was no gold, there were no mines, there are no mines, and it's all a bunch of pap. Just what the Peraltas preferred people to think, while they were busy mining.

I was talking with an old timer in Tempe who had a long, white beard and had lived in Arizona some eighty years.

"I know about the Dutchman! He was nothing but a thief. Yeh, he had everybody fooled about his mine. He never had any mine in the Superstitions. There's no gold up there. That Dutchman was robbing Mexican pack trains and stealing their gold. He'd sneak into the Superstitions, rob the Mexicans of their gold, hide it, and sneak back. Used to come back into Pheonix somewhere on North Central. But he never had no mine."

Now the interesting thing here is, the assertion that

Mexicans had gold. Where were these Mexican pack trains coming from, and going to? Mines, of course.

Of the mines the Peraltas operated, a small number were in the Superstition Mountains near what is now Apache Junction, and have been positively identified as old Spanish or Mexican workings. But the majority of the gold mines were in an area forty miles northwest of there, at the western edge of the Superstition Mountain *Range*, near the town of Carefree. It is this area where the Peraltas had located their richest mines, the mines north of Sombrero Mountain, north of Needle Mountain. In almost all of the gold stories which came out of Mexico, the rich mines were to the north of these mountains. Sombrero Mountain was not located until recently, and Needle Mountain was erroneously thought to be Weaver's Needle. But Needle Mountain is Picacho Butte, which is now called Pinnacle Peak.

The Peraltas were among the only people to move through the Superstition Mountains because even today, the Superstitions are something you go "around," not "through." They're so rugged and dry that they're nearly impossible to travel, even on foot, which is perfect for someone who is experienced and wants to travel undetected. For someone who wants to transport gold back to Sonora. Even the Apaches seldom went into the Superstitions during the early eighteen hundreds; they were camped much lower in the nearby valleys and along the rivers where there was water, grass for their animals, and game. And Apaches were something to be avoided, at all costs.

The story of mining in Arizona takes a new dimension and really gets going after the Mexican American War, when Americans began to find and operate mines in Arizona, and spread the word. When Americans began to do in the open, what the Peraltas had been doing quietly and secretly. When Americans began writing history. The Mexican American War must have been something the Peraltas saw coming, way ahead of time, if they had any political acumen whatsoever. And it could be easily shown that they did, since they had managed to survive the Mexican Revolution with their mining operations intact, if not stronger. But it is not only the Mexican American War directly that caused the decline of the Peralta mining operations, it is also the chain of events which the coming of the war must have set into motion. These events, coupled with some unfortunate circumstances, totally destroyed the Peralta operations in Arizona, and they were never able to regain control of their mines again. It was during these years that a German immigrant by the name of Jacob Waltz first came to America, arriving in Baltimore, Maryland in 1839. Political turmoil in Germany was high at the time with considerable revolutionary transition in the German States. Waltz had probably learned his first valuable lessons in politics, lessons which would serve him well, later, when he arrived in Arizona.

Chapter 4

The End of Mexican Control

Don Miguel Peralta II was a man of great wisdom, of great daring, and of great spirit. From a family with a tradition of accomplishments which held respect through two generations of kings in Spain, Don Miguel had not only kept the favor of at least one King of Spain but had demonstrated his keen political ability in establishing a similar rapport with Santa Anna. The question of how he managed to keep control over the family mines through the transition of power away from Spain to the Mexican revolutionaries and Santa Anna is an interesting one. One could ask, who did he support? Could he have remained neutral? Maybe he bought himself clear of it, or maybe he defended his holdings with the men he commanded, keeping a low profile in Mexico like he did with his mining operations in Arizona. There are some stories which claim that he sent gold back to the mines in Arizona to hide it until after the revolution. Regardless of the answer, he obviously knew how to conduct himself politically. Born in 1781, just after the American Revolution, he probably had learned to watch this new country closely, as a child, maybe in amazement. His father died when he was seven. He would have been forty at the time of the Mexican Revolution. In the early 1840's, Don Miguel Peralta II would have been in his early sixties, and would also have seen the inevitable: the United States would soon expand again and take control of Arizona. Don Miguel was going to have to make some decisions about the fate of his mines. Not being a U.S. citizen, he would no longer be able to mine them if Mexico lost title to the territory.

So Don Miguel had to change the operations. And he did what anyone would be compelled to do under the circumstances: launch an intensive mining effort on as large a scale as possible, get as much gold as possible, and then get out, hopefully hiding the location of the mines until the proper political arrangements could be made to operate them again.

The dangers were great, as he would certainly have known, but there was no choice.

So they went and approximately four hundred strong, north into Arizona. Don Miguel would have led his men up southern Arizona into the Superstitions and probably past Petroglyph Rock where one of the master maps was located. Some of the men would have been ordered to stay and work the mines in the nearby proximity, but most of the men would have traveled northwest to the richer mines past Sombrero Mountain and Sombrero Butte. The route would have been to the north and west, possibly through what is now Apache Junction or possible along a higher trail in the mountains, through what is now Usuary Pass, across the Salt River and on up into the Verde River country. Because of the size of their party, they couldn't have moved into the Verde River area without being detected by the Apaches. This was a tremendous danger. It is said that the Peraltas had been able to work in small numbers with relatively little trouble from the Apaches, but Don Miguel must have known that this would be too much.

As their fate worsened with exposure to Apaches, the danger deepened as they moved up Camp Creek from the Verde River. The steep, narrow canyon which tended to the north offered an easy, well hidden trail in, but what about later, when they would try to come back out? It would have been a troubled face which led the men in, but the only way to follow the landmarks was to follow the trail. It is well known that the Apaches camped along the Verde River in great numbers, and it is likely that the Peraltas had seen them, and vice versa.

Once into the area, the mining camps were set up. Some to work the placer in the various washes, some to work the tunnels and shafts, and some to operate the arrastras to process the gold. Ore was transported to the arrastras on the previously constructed trails using mules. And while this work was in progress, the Peraltas may have engraved their maps of the rich area into stone tablets to enable future generations to find the mines. It is also possible that they already possessed the stone tablets and had obtained them from the Jesuits.

A third possibility is that the expedition was launched with the assistance of Jesuits themselves, returning for their church treasures and gold which had been hidden in 1747. Whatever the case, a large mining and expedition party went north into the Apache lands near the Verde River and beneath the Apache Thunder God. The stone tablets, however, were either produced or carried by those who went in.

There is little to confirm the precise year when the journey into the area took place, one account says as early as 1841. It was probably closer to 1843, and may have been as late as 1846. The question is, how long did the Peralta miners work the area? How much gold did they prepare for their farewell journey back into Sonora? And were they assisted in any way by Jesuits? They may have worked the area several years, and may have only worked it for one year. They may have had enough ore to process without having to do too much more hard rock mining. But the location of their activity, coupled with the size of their party, marked the beginning of doom for the Peraltas and whoever went with them.

Several of the mines were located directly beneath and across the wash from the Apache Thunder God. And the Apaches had already grown to hate the Spanish. The Peraltas may have been an exception to this hate by working quietly in small numbers, but the large size of their party may have changed the feelings of the Apaches. At any rate, there were warnings. Again, the Apaches were not going to allow their Thunder God to be disturbed or destroyed. And again, they attacked.

A few mules were killed and there were signs that the Apaches were angered. The Peraltas were offending the Apaches by taking gold out of the ground right there, right in front of the Stone Head, but the Peraltas continued working the area. Then a few men were killed and the Apaches gathered in greater numbers. An attack was certain to be launched, and the Peraltas, in haste, ordered the men to pack the gold and prepare to leave immediately.

But it was too late. Some of the men were attacked and killed where they worked at the mines and the Apaches threw their bodies and tools into the shafts and tunnels. But most of the Mexican miners made it back to join the main group in the lower canyon and they all fled the area. They headed down Camp Creek toward the Verde River and they were barely under way when the Apaches attacked from the rear. They fought on the run with their mules behind them and the Apaches shot arrows and hit the mules. The heavily laden mules dropped with their bags of gold and the Peraltas kept going, trying desperately to escape. But when they got to a place where the canyon widened, the Apaches attacked from above on the ridges. The Peraltas ran first to one side, then across to the other side as the hail of arrows came down upon them from one side, and then the other. Back and forth they ran and the mules and men were slaughtered in great numbers. The bags of gold dropped into the bed of Camp Creek along with countless bodies of Mexicans. Those who escaped were continually chased by the Apaches who were determined to kill them all. The battle lasted for two to three days.

A few made their way back up the Verde and back into the high Superstitions where the other mining parties were working. But the Apaches attacked there too. Again a slaughter ensued. The men tried to escape to the south, following the trail back toward Sonora, and the Apaches chased them and killed them. Their bags of gold and stone tablets were scattered with their bodies all the way from Camp Creek to the area near the location of the present day city of Florence. The date on one of the stone tablets, discovered approximately one hundred years later, reads 1847. These tablets are now in the Mesa Southwest Museum. There was only one believed survivor: Manuel Peralta.

Confident that their slaughter was complete, the Apaches then set out to conceal the mines in order to make sure that no white man would ever be able to find them. To make sure that no one would find the gold. They had learned that men would always come back for the gold mines, and it was the only way to protect their Thunder God.

They sent their squaws and young boys, who worked from one moon to the next at hiding every trace of every mine, but one. It was high on the side of a canyon, so remote, so hard to see that they left it untouched. But the concealment of the other mines was thorough. All tools, gold and bodies were buried and cactus and bushes were planted. The ore and tailings were scattered and buried. Not a trace remained visible.

Little did they know that the one mine they left exposed was destined to become the most sought after and famous mine in the entire history of Arizona.

Pen Dot Drawing of the Dutchman by Kelley Sands

Chapter 5

The Man in the Shadows: 1848 to 1862

The year 1848 was an eventful year in terms of mining in the American Southwest. The Apaches had recently massacred the Peraltas, the United States had signed a treaty with Mexico ending the war, and gold had been discovered in California. The treaty paved the way west and the gold rush was on. In that same year, 1848, among the first to travel west was a German immigrant by the name of Jacob Waltz.

It is ironic that gold was discovered in California on January 24, 1848, and that the treaty ending the Mexican-American War was signed on February 2nd, just nine days later. In the haste of the matter, the United States had acquired only the part of Arizona *north* of the Gila River. This turned out to be a gross error when it was learned that a significant portion of the southern trail to California lay *south* of the Gila. It also came to light that there were significant mineral resources south of the Gila including gold, silver and copper. It took the United States five years to correct the problem but it was finally done with the Gadsden Purchase in 1853 at a cost of ten million dollars.

But this oversight didn't stop Americans from treading Mexican soil to get to California. It is estimated that between 1848 and 1853 some thirty thousand to sixty thousand emigrants traveled the southern route through Arizona. Thousands moved through the Arizona territory without finding or even *looking*, for gold *there*. Besides, they were formally in Mexico on much of the trail. It was just like the thousands in California who trod the ground in the area of Sutter's Mill and never saw the flakes of gold where they lay in plain sight on the ground. Until someone noticed. Until someone *told them* there was gold in the area. *Then* they started looking.

Jacob Waltz was believed to have worked two other gold strikes in the South between the years of 1841 and 1847, the first gold rushes in the United States. These little known strikes occurred in North Carolina in 1826, northern Georgia in 1828, and spread to the Appalachian Mountains well into the 1840's. These strikes were not well known, yet they yielded enough gold that the United States government set up a mint in Charlotte, North Carolina, in 1837 and another one in Dahlonega, Georgia, in 1838. Five million dollars in gold was coined in the Charlotte mint alone, prior to the Civil War. Jacob Waltz would have been a late comer among the many German immigrants known to have engineered and worked the mines and probably didn't bring much of that to the mint. But, nonetheless, Waltz would have learned two things: gold mining, and northern-southern strife.

This flash of yellow fire had even the dead back on their feet. Although the actual strike occured on January 24, 1848, it was late summer and early fall before the news hit the streets in the Eastern cities. And it was 1849 when the largest westward migration in United States hit the territories of the West.

Jacob Waltz was in Natchez, Mississippi, when news of the California gold strike hit the south like a bright yellow forest fire. People went out of control, they left their homes, they packed their things, and they headed west. Jacob Waltz had filed a declaration of citizenship with the Adams County Circuit Court on November 12th, 1848, but there was no further effort in the matter after that date. Waltz had gone west.

It was a different approach from that of the Spaniards. It was a different approach from that of the Mexicans. The United States government would point the way to the gold and open the doors, and the miners would pay the price of finding it and fighting for it and the lands where it was buried. It had worked before, and it would work again. And the gold, eventually but surely, would wind up in the mint.

He would have taken the southern route from Mississippi, going through Texas and the New Mexico Territory which included Arizona. He would have traveled west through Arizona on the trail near the Gila River in the winter of 1848-1849, the same approximate time that any surviving Peralta miners, including Manuel, would have been traveling south through the same territory. The trail west went through both newly acquired U.S. territory and Mexico land. What's important here is whether Jacob Waltz met with a Peralta, or someone, or anyone having knowledge of the Peralta mines north of the Gila River. It certainly could have happened. Whether it happened or not, one thing is known: the Lost Dutchman mine was an old Jesuit, Peralta or Spanish mine.

There is no physical record of the activities of Jacob Waltz between his departure from Mississippi near the end of 1848 and his appearance in California in 1860. On July 24, 1860 he is known to have been a day laborer in Azusa Township in the County of Los Angeles, but his whereabouts prior to that are purely a speculative matter. One thing to be sure of, though, is that Jacob Waltz was in active pursuit of gold.

There are only two places Waltz could have been mining or prospecting prior to his appearance in Los Angeles County: the northern California gold strike area near San Francisco, and the southern Arizona/northern

Mexico area near the Southern Trail. Waltz may not have learned about the Peralta mines as he passed through the area on the Southern Trail, in which case he would have certainly been in northern California. Further, Waltz could have learned something about the Spanish mines north of the Gila but been so anxious to get to California that he didn't linger, continued the trip to northern California, and simply remembered about the Spanish mines when he returned to Arizona some years later. This prior knowledge of Spanish mines may have enabled him to locate the old workings and thus, his famous mine.

But there is another possibility. There are stories about Jacob Waltz and a "partner" by the name of Jacob Weiser having saved one Miguel Peralta's life in a fiesta brawl over a card game. The stories tell of Miguel being stabbed by a gambler in a fight and of Weiser breaking a bottle over the head of the gambler. Waltz and Weiser then are said to have taken Miguel to his hacienda somewhere near the location of the brawl in Sonora. Having saved Miguel's life and striking a friendship, the story goes that the three men made a partnership to return to the Peralta mines north of the Gila to bring out gold, gold from mines which Miguel could no longer work because of the Guadalupe-Hidalgo Treaty.

Some accounts of these stories do not date these events and some date them in the 1860's. But if this happened, it most likely happened in the winter of 1848-1849. Once again, the possibilities abound. If Miguel Peralta survived *the Apache massacre, then it is possible that he met up with Waltz and they worked together. They may have worked mines together for several years, and they may even have gone to southern California together. But more than likely, this is not the case. Because Waltz would not have gone to California at all if he had a rich mine in Arizona.*

In all probability, Jacob Waltz learned something about the Spanish mines as he traveled the Southern Trail through Arizona and Mexico, but kept going and went to northern California. Then he probably went to southern California when news of that strike hit northern California in either 1853 or 1854.

The gold strike in California proved out and the U.S. government opened a mint in San Francisco in 1852. Between April and December of 1854, more than four million dollars was coined-- all in gold. The government had experienced the same problem shipping gold from California all the way across the frontier to the Philidelphia Mint that the Spaniards had experienced in getting gold out of Arizona: Indians, robbers and fraud. Only worse, since everyone knew about it. And San Francisco proper also had its problems. There were tens of thousands of people with no place to live. There were hundreds of murders and virtually none of them solved or punished. And public records were a mess.

The fate of Miguel Peralta II is similar to that of other people in Arizona and California during the time. Accounts differ. Some say he died in the massacre by the Apaches, and some say he survived. Again, ironically, an account of a Don Miguel Peralta II shows him in San Diego, California in 1853, the same year of the gold strike in that area. Waltz is known to have been there some years later, but the date of his arrival is not specifically known. Speculatively, Waltz was there in 1853. But the fact that this account of Miguel Peralta II in San Diego in 1853 comes forward as part of a fraudulent effort to revive and enforce the Peralta Land Grant in 1867 raises some question as to the validity of the account.

The answers as to the relationship of these bits of story are crucial to the extent, if any, of the relationship of any of the Peraltas to Jacob Waltz prior to the Civil War. But it is possible that he learned of the mines from another source while crossing Arizona: Indians.

Waltz would have crossed an area heavily inhabited by Pima and Maricopa Indians, and somewhat inhabited by Apaches. Waltz is remembered to have commented once in his later years that he had often considered a life with the Pimas, it was so peaceful. This comment likens Waltz to the earliest "mountain man" type of pioneer. These early explorers often earned respect from Indians rather than offend them. And he may have learned the ways of many Indians, including the Apaches on his journey along the southern route. If he did, it was certainly a wise endeavor, for whether or not it assisted him directly in discovering the one Spanish mine which the Indians did not conceal, it certainly would have assisted him in later travels through lands controlled by the Apaches. Other travelers, especially in groups, were viewed differently, as either settlers or armies. That was trouble. "Mountain men" moved on, like the Apache. To the Apache, it was the difference between exploration and exploitation. The difference between living with the land, and conquering it.

Waltz in his later life never mentioned having known any Peraltas, but he didn't mention anything about any of his other mining experiences prior to 1860, either. So this doesn't totally exclude the possibility. He did say that he stumbled upon the old workings as a result of prospecting placer deposits in some of the nearby washes, but it's a curious coincidence that he had crossed the lands of the Peraltas many years before and that he also referred to the mine as an old Spanish working. Further, Lost Dutchman Mine maps contain many of the same landmarks that their maps did. Of course, Waltz would have seen the same landmarks, since they are there and he was there, but did he know about any of them before he saw them? That's the question. And a hard one to answer. Specific knowledge of his wherabouts in the early 1850's is crucial to understanding this part of his life and whether it had any direct bearing on his mining activities later in Arizona. To date, there is none. This may have been intentional on his part. Waltz had probably learned what the Spaniards knew, what the Jesuits knew, what the Peraltas knew, and what any miner should have known: keep your mouth shut about gold. Waltz further, being a man of wit, must also have learned that a man must talk some, simply to get by. This is why he later talked in riddles. To talk and yet reveal, nothing. Waltz was a man who stayed in the shadows.

Waltz did, however, make a sworn statement to the effect that he had been in California at least one year prior to July 19, 1861, and in the United States continually for the previous five years from that date. This is of record in Los Angeles County Court in his certificate of citizenship which bears this date. He would have been fifty one years old. It is purposeful that he claimed his citizenship on July 19th when the Civil War started on April 12th of that same year. He must have received news of the secession of South Carolina in 1860, and Mississippi was not far behind. He quickly sent to Natchez for his "Intention to Become a Citizen" papers and the Clerk of the Circuit Court of Adams County certified them on January 15, 1861. Waltz received the papers just in time, because the mail service from the Confederacy was suspended that same summer. Further, coinage operations were suspended at the mint in Dahlonega, Georgia, and also at the mint in Charlotte, North Carolina (which the Confederates converted into an army headquarters).

Waltz narrowly escaped the citizenship quandary through quick political prowess, and then, in that same year, he was faced with another serious threat: natural disaster. There were a series of floods in southern California during the winter of 1861-1862. Water was several feet deep in Anaheim and the San Gabriel River became a thundering torrent. Boulders the size of houses thundered down its banks and the raging river totally destroyed the mining camps and placer claims where Waltz apparently worked. The precious sands had been ripped up and scattered throughout a huge flood plain, and the miners must have looked on afterward in total dismay. As one door closes, another opens, and shortly thereafter the thunderous roar was that of feet on their way to yet another placer strike: the lower Colorado River area near Yuma, Arizona. Waltz had gone to Arizona.

Waltz never filed a claim in Yuma County. But Waltz is believed to have been in Yuma County in 1862 because he is reported to have told a census taker in 1864 that he had lived in Arizona for two years. Also, there is an account by a local La Paz resident to the effect that Waltz's first mining days in the 1860's were spent in La Paz. He may have crossed the Colorado River at the same place he crossed on his way into California, although the date of his first crossing is still in the air.

It should be noted here that according to Book 3, Deeds and Claims, La Paz, May 2, 1863, pp. 99-100, Records of Yuma County, there is record of the Plomosa Placers, a group of dry diggings, and Peraltas were listed as claimants, as well as one Felipe Gonzales. Again, the paths of Waltz and the Peraltas cross. One story describes Miguel as being in California and then coming to La Paz, and further asserts that this was the first Peralta mine in Arizona. Well, it may have been the first "recorded" Peralta mine in Arizona after the territory became part of the United States, and it may be that it took some time for some of the Peraltas to become citizens, maybe in California. Waltz had done that, too. If one of the Peraltas came from the Southern California gold strike when he heard news of the strike at La Paz, then it's entirely possible that Waltz and the Peralta got news of the strike at the same time, and may have even traveled in the same party.

By this time the Civil War was raging as hot and heavy as the San Gabriel River and the Yankees had pulled their troops out of Arizona to reinforce the war effort elsewhere. The result: the Apache Indians interpreted this withdrawal as defeat, and the "victorious" Apaches were now even more dangerous to encounter (if that can be possible).

Waltz went north through Arizona to the area of Wickenburg undaunted by the danger of Indians. There were other miners who made the same trip and the gaze of Waltz upon the rest of them would have been that of, "I know more than all of you put together." And the return glances, if dared, would have been skating pretty thin. You can bet that Waltz, having survived the Appalachian Mountains and those men, the Arizona Territory including

Mexico and those men (and Indians), San Francisco and those men, Los Angeles county and those men, Yuma County and those men (Indians again), and now the trip to Wickenburg, was one clever and tough Dutchman. Not to mention what he knew about gold and a man's mouth.

Chapter 6

Claims

Waltz did, however, file claims in 1863, 1864 and 1865. But there were no more claims filed by him. Ever. It is possible that no *prior* claims had been filed because Waltz had not been a citizen until after 1861. It is interesting to note the names of the claims: The Gross Lode, September 21, 1863, named after a fellow German immigrant who was also a claimant, the Big Rebel, September 14, 1864, named after the Civil War on behalf of the South, and the General Grant Lode, December 27, 1865, named after the victorious Civil War general from the North. Emboldened by citizenship, Waltz filed these claims, but the importance of political thought is obvious. Yankee troops had been pulled out of Arizona to fight elsewhere, and it's possible that not only the Apaches, but Waltz too, interpreted this as a sign of defeat.

Waltz signed his name on March 11, 1864 to a petition to Governor John N. Goodwin asking the governor for a militia to protect miners from Indian attacks. Waltz might have named the Big Rebel as a sign of allegiance in case the rebels won. Maybe he just felt deserted by the Yankees, who certainly made life tougher for those in Arizona when it came to the Indians. Two of his earlier "partners" had died unnatural deaths in 1870, one by Apaches and one on the Hassayampa River. It could have been that the governor hadn't helped the miners that he named it the Big Rebel. It could have also been that Waltz felt that the government didn't care about independent miners. Maybe it had something to do with the Indians themselves. But whatever the case, he switched his political bent when he named his next claim after General Grant. Maybe it was because he saw the coming of the Eastern money, armed with their teams of lawyers and engineers. It may have been similar to the carpetbaggers who went south. One thing stands out: Waltz knew that politics had a lot to do with mining, and there were many things which happened in this boom area in just a few short years with regard to claims and their status under the law.

It is likely that no *subsequent* claims were filed by Waltz due to his experiences in the Walnut Grove District (south of Prescott) and the Pioneer-Walker District. Details about Waltz in the area are scattered and few. Waltz had four partners on the Gross Lode claim area and one of them,

William Gross, sold out to two other men for a hundred dollars. The new "partners" were Gideon Brooke and J.B. Slack. Slack was a former Kentucky sheriff who'd come west in the Mexican War of 1846-1848. Brooke later became Deputy Recorder of the Walker Quartz Mining district in 1881, and Slack was later implicated in the great Arizona Diamond Swindle of 1871-1872. In 1865 both men refiled their shares of the Gross Lode, although a twisty tangle begins to surround the mine. In June of 1864, one third interest in the mine was transferred by Isaac Bradshaw to William Reed. Bradshaw? The name just pops up, and then a Robert Groom staked a claim adjacent to the site, and then three additional locations were recorded in quick succession: Henry Clifton, a deputy recorder, L. Thrift, and Charles Noble.

Waltz, as well as his interest, disappeared from the Gross Lode. With even the deputy recorder jumping in, it's no surprise. Something else disappeared, too: the location of the claim. No one knows where it was, except that it was once described as having been twelve miles from the Walker placer diggings. With all these men who owned it, the filings, re-filings, transfers, publicly recorded documents and stories, it's gone. Only it's not gone. It's just lost.

Whether the mine is worth looking for or not, there's a story here of one little mine and many men after it. Maybe Waltz noticed that by recording their claim they wound up with even a deputy recorder chasing the gold. Maybe Waltz noticed other things, too, about mining claims, like maybe that things could get unclear just as fast as a deluge could muddy up stream. The deluge, of course, consisted of men and their paper.

There was some reason for the paper boom in the area. Arizona had been the proving of some of the richest and most sensational mines in the United States. Like so many stories which will repeat in this book, the next will resemble the last. Henry Wickenburg, who had changed both his first and last name (formerly Heinrich Heinsel), prospected the area near the Hassayampa River along with several other prospectors. The men were camped, presumeably together, but apparently Wickenburg had prospected alone in the moment that he discovered free gold on the ground. Numerous nuggets. It is said that he told the other men in the camp of the find and showed them some of the gold. It is also said that they didn't believe him, or his gold, at that precise moment. Later, however, they changed their belief and declared themselves partners on Wickenburg's claims.

Waltz named his claims after the Civil War and Wickenburg named his after a vulture. There's something in common here. As if coming to a calling, the vultures were all over Wickenburg's claim like Alfred Hitchcock's movie *The Birds*. A number of men claimed to be equal partners and the labyrinths of litigation resemble a hedge maze: properly designed, there's no way out. The Vulture

Mine turned out to have the richest ore of any mine ever discovered in the world, and the legal charges, counter-charges and trials reached national publicity. Let's not forget that the United States government had just emerged from a devastating civil war and desperately needed gold to mint money. The population at large was too smart to accept paper money instead of gold coins for payment, and when they did it was only upon the belief that the gold was "in reserve" to back the paper. So the war had to be paid for, in gold (this eventually watered down to percentages, then to silver and silver certificates, and then to nothing but empty promises).

Wickenburg had initially worked the claim himself, alone. He hauled the ore to the Hassayampa (about six miles away) where he built an arrastre for crushing the ore. This was the same method the Spanish had used for centuries in Arizona, and his yield was so sensational that another gold rush got started.

Wickenburg realized the extent of the claim and expanded the operation. He sold ore to some, and let them transport it by mule to his arrastre and then rented them the arrastre. But others built their own, and within a year there were some forty arrastres along the river. The town of Wickenburg sprang up and by 1866 there was a 20-stamp mill. The German immigrant who'd arrived in 1862 was now operating a mine which produced $3,000 a day.

While the arrastres and stamp mills ground the ore, the

attorneys ground the paper. By 1879, both were still grinding busily away. The attorneys produced scatological paper and the mine produced $21,000 per week in gold. The Vulture, and the vultures, in spite of the wealth, were too much for Henry Wickenburg, and he tried to sell four-fifths interest in the mine to a New York capitalist for $85,000. A strange sum for a mine which was producing at the time, over $1,000,000 per year. Due to legal entanglements, the transaction was never "legally" consummated. The attorneys, and let's not forget there's a United States government with its role in the matter, had dug in deeper than even the original claimant, and the gold wound up in the mint, and probably quite a bit of it via the pockets of what we now call red tape.

Getting out of the "offices" and into the streets, the years between 1865 and 1880 illustrated the value of the law with over four hundred murders, hijackings, shootings, stock swindles, fraud, bribes and all those "cleanly things" which came to an end only when two natural disasters hit: a flood which took the town and a fault which took the mine.

The flood of 1890 was massive and substantially worsened in effect due to the collapse of the Walnut Grove Dam, constructed above Wickenburg in an area used for recreation at the time. The raging Hassayampa killed some eighty persons and ranches, mills, mines and towns were ruined.

The fault in the Vulture Mine had been discovered at a

depth of some twelve hundred feet, and marked the end of the vein of gold. The ore of the mine had gotten richer as the men had gone deeper, until they got to the fault. They dug all around and mineralogists and engineers could not find where the rich vein continued. Like a manned process of natural erosion, the rock pillars which provided the foundations for the numerous levels above were taken out a little at a time as ore, and processed to finance the continued efforts to find the vein. They chipped away at the pillars until one day, with a full shift working, over a hundred men died in a massive collapse.

The Vulture was dead and Henry Wickenburg retired to a small house on his property. A man who'd stood up to unceasing litigation, a man who'd discovered the richest ore in the world, Henry Wickenburg was thought of by many as a defeated man. Maybe he even thought that of himself. Maybe he didn't. The answer may exist only in the mind of the body that pulled the trigger which ended his life on his eighty-eighth birthday at the very spot where he'd first camped on the banks of the Hassayampa River. Henry Wickenburg was found dead with a bullet in his brain and a pistol in his hand in 1905. That to some means suicide. But who could really know?

There are other possibilities. For one thing, The Vulture was not dead. And presumeably, neither were the "vultures." Within less than three years, the mine was re-opened. Between 1908 and 1915 the mine produced close to $2,000,000. Even the old, rock buildings and houses were run through the mill having a value of $20 per ton. True to the adage, vultures will eat anything. But one question remains: did the vultures wait for Henry Wickenburg to die? Did they circle above him, watching, waiting, watching? Or did they kill the man even though he was old, the man who must have hated their black hearts and souls, the man who'd fought their lurking presence from the first day the real bird cast its shadow upon him. It was worked again during the Depression. It was worked again in the 1950's. And yet today, someone must claim some title to it, and maybe it's questionably so, maybe it's not. Someday, someone will find the lost vein. And the vultures will return.

I met a man recently who'd been to the old site of Rich Hill, a boom area of the 1860's near Stanton, Arizona. "There were twenty seven graves at the old cemetary which itself, was on top of a hill. You know how many of them died a natural death? Two."

What happened to Jacob Waltz on the seemingly insignificant scale of the Gross Lode, and what happened to Henry Wickenburg on the grand scale of the Vulture Mine, happened en masse among the many prospectors and claims in the area. Some say it was the result of "lode claims" as opposed to the previous "placer claims," their reasoning being that lode claims required heavy equipment to crush rock and dynamite to blast, and thus heavy capital investment to operate. Some said that a miner would go broke trying to get enough yield out of a lode claim, even worse, starve trying. Henry Wickenburg didn't, but that's beside the point. For whatever political reason (probably more oriented toward dishonesty), the meeting of the first Territorial Legislature in the Autumn of 1864 marked the end of the autonomy of the old mining districts and the beginning of a rush of prospectors into the county claiming up as much prospective gold lands as they could survey and stake. Claims floated through the streets like so many leaves in a New England autumn wind. And the hard-headed industrialists from the East sent in mining experts to set up large scale mining operations. Many of the smaller claim holders may have been anxious to liquidate their claims, especially the ones who had fictitious or borderline ore. Many of them with truly valuable claims may have been forced into selling, either through the filing requirements concerning assessments and all the tangles of claim legality/validity, or through less "up and up" methods. In any case, thousands of claims were bought, sold or traded. Placer mines in the piney areas near Prescott faded and miners wandered down into the Wickenburg settlement where "lode mining" emerged as the "thing of the future."

The real miners had learned, or they died in the lesson, that a man had to protect and hold what was his, on his own. The law wasn't going to protect a claim or a miner. Lawyers weren't going to do anything but secure holdings for those with big money and the corrupt, and no one could handle the Indians. Waltz and others had signed that petition to Governor Goodwin in 1864 requesting the formation of a militia but it was not formed. Many died at the hands of the Indians, and many Indians died too. They were all trying to hold onto something for which ownership on paper was twisty, and on the ground was as deadly as a rattlesnake. A smart man kept to himself. And no one should be surprised that Waltz filed no more claims. A quiet man.

Many of the miners wound up working for the Vulture and other mines in the area. Some have asserted that Waltz had been one of them, and that his gold which he spent in Phoenix years later was simply that which he high-graded from the Vulture. But more than likely, the spirit of Waltz was that of a man who'd follow his heart. And seeing men pull gold from the Vulture was only one aspect of what Waltz had seen in the area. He'd been in mining areas throughout the South, throughout California and over much of Arizona. It was some of the same lesson. Coming late was not the way to mine gold, nor was there anything in working someone else's mine. Waltz was too proud, too independent to have worked at the Vulture. And if he did, it would have been a situation of regret for him. Highgrading by Waltz is unlikely, and was brought up primarily by those who did not believe that the Lost Dutchman Mine existed, as an explanation for Waltz's possession of gold in Phoenix.

He was not a thief, he was a miner. With a mine. And a heart. And considerable wisdom about the fate of the Wickenburg area.

At least one other man in the area must have seen the same things: Jack Swilling, a manager of the Corbin Mill which shut down due to a lack of water. In the faltering of small mines, the business of merchants and saloonkeepers flourished. Men must eat, and at the time most of the supplies came from California. Swilling, who had been a guide for the Walker party, conceived of a plan to irrigate land along the Salt River for farming, much as the Hohokams had done centuries earlier. The government had made a key contribution to the value of his irrigation company, not regarding the value of water, not regarding the value of grains, but regarding ownership of land: The Homestead Act.

In September of 1867, a number of men left Wickenburg for what is now the city of Phoenix. A number of German immigrants quickly constructed a canal which was named the Dutch Ditch. Whether Waltz left Wickenburg with Swilling, or later, is not known. But what is known is that Jacob Waltz in 1868 took up a homestead of 160 acres of land which was watered by the Dutch Ditch. Further, his neighbors were the Starars, also German immigrants. By 1870, Waltz had filed a $400 assessment for improvements to his homestead but he never proved his land claim to obtain a deed thereto. The Starars did. If Waltz's motive in filing the Homestead was to get land, rather than to farm, then he'd been one to see the nature of the greatest source of revenue and profit which Arizona ever enjoyed: Land development and sales.

The matter of the ownership of the several homesteads filed near the Starars, and including the Waltz homestead, is a curious one. Because when the railroad first got to Phoenix it is a well known fact that the first people on it were land speculators. It's curious that Waltz never perfected the title to his homestead and never received title, yet he somehow transferred it, or quitclaimed it to the Starars in exchange for the promise of shelter and medical care for the rest of his life.

The homestead in general was easy to enter into, in terms of filing for 160 acres, but there were numerous complications in obtaining title. There were filing requirements, and sometimes twisting details which required the services of an attorney to assure full satisfaction of all the requirements set forth by the government. Many who filed for homesteads and improved the land were later beat out of it. Or simply lost their chance to title by not filing as they were required to do. Large companies and land barons often became experts, and wound up with huge holdings through the paperwork. Big lumber companies in the 1860's and 1870's used to bring elderly ladies to Oregon from the East in considerable numbers for vacations, and then get them to sign the homestead papers.

They had a team of lawyers which processed all the required filings and documentation until title was obtained. In this manner, huge forests were acquired. There's some sense to it, since paper was growing to be the most coveted possession of man, replacing even gold for money. And working the paper which represented land and mining claims was to become more important and rewarding than working the land or claims themselves. This was contrary to both the mining law and the homestead act, which were designed to allow the common men to obtain enduring title to land by working it, whether farming or mining.

It's curious that Andrew Starar failed to pay taxes on Waltz's homestead and lost title in 1886. Men were making money from land in Phoenix, but it wasn't the Starars nor the Waltz's. One thing was surely set in Waltz's mind: Nobody was going to make money from his gold mine except himself.

Several things are obvious through the course of Waltz's move from the Walnut Grove District to the future site of Phoenix. Waltz traveled through the area north of Phoenix, Waltz left a mess of mining and men, Waltz traveled down through the area north of Phoenix and may have seen evidence of old Spanish or Mexican workings. Waltz filed a homestead on 160 acres of land in 1868 (some date this differently by a few years), deeded the homestead to his neighbor Starar on August 8th, 1878, along with everything there of record which he owned, and in 1880 lived on the same quarter section of land with Henry Ewing. It doesn't matter when he homesteaded, or what he farmed, or what he sold in eggs (except maybe that he met Julia Thomas). He was a miner at heart. And what he did at mining is not obvious. Purposely so.

Ewing is significant because on August 15th, 1878, ownership of the Valenciana Mine is listed as a relocation in partnership with one of the old mine's original discoverers: Miguel Peralta. The mine was located in the Black Canyon Mining District in Yavapai County. Peralta and Ewing. Something was going on.

Whatever Waltz was up to, there was no one who knew. But the fact that he had once again come into contact with one of the Peraltas or at least with Ewing who knew a Peralta in association with "an old Spanish working" is an indication that it wasn't farming. As surely as some of the richest discoveries in the 1870's and 1880's proved out to be old Spanish or Mexican mines, Waltz's famous Lost Dutchman mine was also an old working.

Waltz in all probability located the mine by putting together some of the stories which came in from the military trails, the stories which came in from Fort McDowell, the stories which came from Mexico, the stories either from or about the Peraltas, and stories from the Indians. He was probably a man who listened, rather than talked. It is ironic that his famous mine was a re-discovered Spanish mine, in effect a "lost mine" when he found it, and that he said later that, "No miner will ever find my mine." His prophecy was correct.

The area of the Lost Dutchman Mine was not discovered by a miner in search of that mine. The discoverer had searched, all right, but the wrong area, the area near Weaver's Needle like everyone else, and then discovered he had the Lost Dutchman Mine in the mid-1980's. He had not known that for years. One of the triggering keys in the realization was the issue of the location of the old military trail, something Waltz had referred to time and time again.

Another connection takes us close. Ewing had worked for Dr. Wilson Walter Jones on his berry farm near Waltz's homestead. Jones had invested in shares of the Vulture Mine, as reported in the *Arizona Sentinel* (Yuma) on August 17, 1878. He had made a small fortune (assumed to be from the Vulture Mine) and had acquired a huge cattle ranch south of Four Peaks, North of Saguaro Lake and between Four Peaks and the Verde River. It was reported that his Mexican wife had received a gift of some $8,000 in gold nuggets from an Apache Indian who had acquired the gold from a surface vein somewhere in the area. Reportedly, it was from the Four Peaks area, but now it can be shown that it was most likely from the Camp Creek area, up Camp Creek from the Verde River, above the old military trail. It was also supposed that the gold came from the mine worked by Jacob Waltz, but in the Superstitions, which everyone interpreted to mean either Four Peaks area or Weaver's Needle. But the mine was up Camp Creek from the Verde River, above the military trail. The point is, Waltz, Jones, Ewing and many others were the seekers of the old mines. And Jones's ranch was very close to the Lost Dutchman Mine. If he had searched for it across the Verde River he may have found it. But the Apaches were there, along the Verde and along Camp Creek. The tops of several hills in the area are covered with pottery, and Indians had lived there for many, many hundreds of years. And one thing the Apaches protected in that area up Camp Creek was their Thunder God. So whatever the Apaches told Jones and/or his wife would have sent them toward Four Peaks or the Superstitions proper, and away from their sacred stone god, and away from the true location of the Dutchman Mine.

This is only one of many relating stories still told today. As the stories about old mines and lost mines whirled through Phoenix through the 1860's, 1870's and 1880's, Waltz may have been one of the few men with the cunning and schrewdness to examine them with respect to the motive of those who told them. There are only three ways he could have found the mine: He could have been prospecting and stumbled into the placer and thus stumbled onto the mine, or he could have been taken to the mine by someone (either Peralta oriented or an Indian), or he could have pieced together some of the stories about lost mines and figured out that so many of them were about the same place and located it by finding the prominant landmarks. Whatever the case, many of the stories were, and are, about the same place. And it's a place which was very well guarded by Apaches.

It is now that the importance of the stories comes to the lead in understanding over a hundred years of mining and searching. The story of the personal life of Waltz in Phoenix is meek from the date he filed his homestead in 1868 through his deeding it away suddenly in August of 1878, and misses the point of what was going on entirely. Stories of gold, and rich discoveries were still going strong during these years, and the fact that Waltz made such a radical change in the domestic status of his affairs in 1878 in Phoenix is indicative that something else had changed first. Something else had been going on all along. We mustn't forget who Jacob Waltz was. We mustn't forget his daring, nor his prowess, nor his ability to live and work secretively. He was a man who needed no one except in sickness, and he knew it.

There's another curious incident surrounding his dwelling at the homestead in Phoenix: The murder of a man in June, 1884 and Waltz's shotgun was determined to be the murder weapon. Waltz was the only witness to give direct testimony to the coroner's jury, and he told of hearing the deceased and another man quarreling, and then the sound of a shot. He denied any knowledge of how his gun had been fired. But it had been. The other man quarreling had been determined by the jury to be the killer, and they further theorized that this man had taken Waltz's gun, shot the victim, and then replaced the gun in Waltz's adobe and fled. Waltz would have been seventy-four at the time. At his turning point, at the time of his contract on his Phoenix holdings in August, 1878, he would have been sixty-eight.

But who were the men? And what did they quarrel over? Or did they even quarrel. Maybe they quarreled with Waltz. What really happened there is not known, but there is a lesson to be taken from it with regard to Jacob Waltz: Someone was shot and killed and Waltz had the cunning to keep out of trouble, even though it was his gun. A good guess is that getting Waltz's gun from him would be harder than getting his gold. A simple look at the epitaphs at the cemetaries near the gold strikes he'd worked for so many years would tell you that. Pedro Ortega, the murdered man, had been a Mexican citizen. If the incident was related to Waltz's gold mine, then Pedro had somehow become an example of a warning mentioned earlier in this book: "This trail is dangerous." Now we are hot upon it.

Chapter 7

The Military Trail and Weaver's Needle

Regardless of how he found the area of "the old Spanish workings," Jacob Waltz found it. And it is believed that he had a partner by the name of Weiser with him.

The initial discovery of gold was the placer in the streambed in the bottom of what is now known as Camp Creek, and at the junction of the bottom of the canyon which comes down from the Apache Thunder God! They camped on the north side, in the thick bushes, where Weiser was said to have brought a small, Dutch oven.

The Indians and Spanish must have also camped at this very spot because the entire hillside is covered with pottery. There were also the remains of what appeared to be pieces of thick cast iron, which very likely could have once belonged to Weiser. This camping spot is also along the trail which led from the Thunder God mines to other mines, and to destinations uncertain at this time. One thing is certain, however. The road was well built at one time, and the old stone supports are still intact, still holding up the road which once had been traveled by the miners of the past.

The military outpost of Fort McDowell was established in 1865 or 1866 to attempt to control the Apaches along the Verde River. Other military outposts were also established, and the military trail which went north from Fort McDowell runs through what is now called Camp Creek. It was named Camp Creek because the soldiers used to camp there on their journeys.

It would not have been safe for travel in the late eighteen hundreds because the Apaches could not be controlled. Even large groups of soldiers would have been risking their lives in this canyon. This was the canyon Waltz prospected and which led him to the "old Spanish working."

Dr. Abram Thorne, a physician at Fort McDowell during the 1860's, had been taken to these old workings but could not find the place again. The story goes that he had saved the life of a young boy who turned out to be the son of an Apache Chief, and he was rewarded by a trip to the rich gold area. Blindfolded as he was taken in, he claimed to have crossed two rivers [or one river twice!], and also as a result of the blindfold slipping or being removed for a moment for him to gather gold, he claimed to have been standing at the bottom of a narrow canyon, and that there seemed to be some sort of ruins on the hillside. As they were returning from the east, he claimed to have seen the tip of a sharp peak to the south.

This would have been Pinnacle Peak. But of primary question is Dr. Thorne's sense of direction. This business about a "sharp peak" was something that would come up again and again. He claimed with some degree of certainty that the mine was within five miles of the peak. Mistakenly thought to be Weaver's Needle.

The greatest single tragedy in the searches and stories about the Lost Dutchman Mine is that so many stories, so many seekers, have misunderstood the relationship of Weaver's Needle to the location of the mine. Especially Julia Thomas.

The fire of the misinterpretation, that the mine was located near Weaver's Needle, stems from two major mistakes. First, it is well known that to get to the mine, Waltz went east and somewhat along the Salt River to get to his mine. He is also known to have said that his mine was at the western end of the Superstition Mountains. So everyone presumed, and they still do, that just because he headed out in this direction that this was the direction of the mine. And because Weaver's Needle had been referred to as a clue, that it was in close proximity of the landmark. Of course, it didn't make sense that when Waltz returned from the mine, he was seen coming into Phoenix on north

Central! That was fobbed off as a ploy to confuse people. Apparently, it was a round trip and quite sensible. So that was one mistake, and second, Julia Thomas and others claimed that Waltz said, "When you're standing at the face of the mine, Weaver's Needle is at four o'clock." And they presumed that he referred to the Needle as a sundial, which at four o'clock indicated the location of the mine by the tip of its shadow. But that's not what he meant. He meant that looking out from the face of the mine, Weaver's Needle is on the horizon at four o'clock! You set your watch with twelve noon as north, and sweep your eyes around to the four o'clock position on the horizon, and you see Weaver's Needle at precisely four o'clock! That's what he meant, navigation time, not a sundial.

So everyone looked in the wrong place. Almost. A few probably found the mine, but none lived to tell it. And their bodies curiously turned up in the Superstition Mountains proper, murder victims with bullets in their heads or their heads removed. Adolph Ruth is probably one such victim who'd actually figured out the clues. Someone was, and maybe still is protecting the true location of the Dutchman Mine, and may have transported bodies to another area entirely.

Waltz and Weiser must have headed up Camp Creek in spite of the danger, either guided by some old map, or stories, or maybe just a hunch. Probably, a story. And they camped at the spot where the small canyons converge,

Plate 9: Rock in the Shape of of a Man's Head

working the placer.

Then Waltz and Weiser worked the deposits up the lesser canyon, heading off Camp Creek from this spot and prospecting northward, until they got to the rich placer directly below the Apache Thunder God (Plate 9: The Rock in the Shape of a Man's Head, Page 89). They would have worked this for a few days, and then gone up, following the rich placer in the hopes of discovering the lode or vein deposit from which it came.

And in this ascent up the thick growth of brush which would have surrounded the old trail, according to the stories, they heard the sound of breaking rock. Two men, whom they thought to be Apaches, worked at the mine. They shot. The other two men died, and turned out to be Mexicans, not Apaches. Waltz said he buried the Mexicans and everything they had at the mine.

It was the one mine which the Apaches had failed to hide, the one mine they'd left open, and it had been found again in spite of the rough terrain.

Who is to say what really happened? And how had the Mexicans found the old workings? Arizona at the time was full of bloodshed between Indians and whites, and that is a moral issue in itself. Who were the Mexicans? Maybe this can be known some day. At this time, it is not.

At any rate, Waltz and Weiser had trouble of their own. They had found a very rich mine, and they had found gold which had been produced and stashed by previous miners.

But Weiser's fate was doomed. Apparently Waltz had returned to town for more equipment and supplies and Weiser, alone, had been attacked by Apaches. In a fabulous tale of survival and daring, Weiser managed to escape with an arrow in the trunk of his body and made his way to the Pimas.

Weiser died but he managed to tell his story, and it was retold by Judge John D. Walker who claimed Weiser gave him detailed directions to the mine. All the stories about Waltz's partner differ, and many claim that he had no partner at all. The matter of Weiser and his story is a matter of speculation.

At any rate, partner or not, Jacob Waltz returned to the mine again and again for gold. And each time, it began with his eastward journey along the Salt River and ended with his appearance in north Phoenix along Central.

Accounts of the amount of gold he brought back differ in all regards. Some say it was in white quartz, some say it was in rose quartz, and some say it was ninety-nine percent pure. Some say he never had a mine, and never had any gold. Julia Thomas believed he did.

Stories of him sneaking to the mine and of killing those who tried to follow him abound. There may be some truth in the killing. One thing seems certain. Waltz had somehow earned the respect of the Apaches to have survived. Maybe it was because he came alone that they didn't kill him. Maybe it was because he fought one-on-one

Plate 10: Stone Tablet (Mesa Southwest Museum) Indicates Church Significance in Spanish Mining

Plate 11: Horse Rock (Man on the Horse)

and earned respect. Apaches were known to be that way, to respect a man with courage enough to stand up alone in the desert.

But Waltz was no fool. He harbored his mules in one part of a cave and slept in the other part, his two room cabin. The cave. That's also an old Spanish working, and the entrance to the cave forks once inside. The fork to the right is a short dead-end room where Waltz slept and any prowler would have been in a cross-fire from Waltz. He was safe there at night. The cave is 1.4 miles from the entrance to one of the Dutchman's mines and the trail would have been rough and well concealed.

He was safe enough, and smart enough, to hold that mine secret until his death. Even then, the clues and maps he gave to those present at his deathbed proved to be too confusing to be of value. "No miner will ever find my mine," Waltz had said, and the search took nearly a hundred years. The discovery? Accidental.

In the words of the modern discover, it was the military trail that clicked the realization into motion. Bill Scovel, in the course of working one of his mines off Seven Springs Road near Carefree had casually asked one of the forest rangers about Camp Creek. "Why do they call it Camp Creek?"

The ranger commented to the effect that "soldiers used to camp there." It clicked in Bill's mind: It was an old military trail. Bill knew the story of the Dutchman Mine, like everyone in the Valley, but it was supposed to be in the Superstitions near Apache Junction. Bill remembered a clue: "From the top of the mine, you can see the old military trail."

He went to the top of the mine and looked out over the desert below. There, clearly and all the way to the Verde River, he could plainly see Camp Creek, the old military trail which had gone from Bloody Basin down to Fort McDowell on the Verde River. A question arose. Where did the military trail go through the Superstitions? Because men had looked for the old military trail for years and never found it in the Superstitions. Bill's old partner, even, who'd searched for the Dutchman Mine for twenty-five years, used to say, "If we could find the old military trail, then maybe we could find the mine."

Bill called a local historian. "Could you tell me where the old military trail went through the Superstitions?"

"You're huntin' the Dutchman Mine, aren't cha!"

Bill was startled and didn't answer.

The historian continued: "The Dutchman did not have a mine in the Superstition Mountains. The military trail did not go through the Superstition Mountains. It went around. Why in the world would they go through them? They went around the Superstition Mountains, on around to Florence Junction and Picket Post."

Bill began to compare the story to the mine he'd been working. The Dutchman had said, "The military trail, a

Plate 12: The Eye of the Needle (Now Pinnacle Peak)

Plate 13: Black Top Mesa (Near Pinnacle Peak)

steep narrow canyon that tends in a north-south direction, full of potholes, a well worn trail, that leads to the mine." Bill followed the trail all the way down to the Verde. It fit. Looking back up toward the mine, he couldn't see the mine. Again, it fit what the Dutchman had said: "From my mine, you can see the military trail but from the trail you can't see the mine which is hidden by the contours of the mountains." It lay hidden.

He went back up to the mine. It was then that he noticed Weaver's Needle. He could see it, clearly, but how could it fit being so far away. Four o'clock! He had it. Every other clue fit. Sombrero Butte (Plate 15, page 101), the Eye of the Needle (Plate 12, page 96), Black Top Hill, and Black Top Mesa (Plate 13, page 97), all to the south of the mine .

In reference to the cave, the two room cabin, the Dutchman had said, "From the hill above the cave, you can see the military trail [Camp Creek]. From here you proceed on down the canyon carefully observing the canyon wall. High on a ridge there is a large formation in the shape of a man's head that looks down on a mine hidden in the bushes below." The Apache Thunder God (Plate 9, page 89).

The story was coming together. And not just the Dutchman's story, but a lot of lost mine stories. Bill followed the canyon down and easily found the stone head, the Apache Thunder God, and looked in the bushes below. There, he found the tunnel. It was all there, just as the

Dutchman had said.

Bill knew then that everything the Dutchman had said had been true. And as he continued investigating all the clues, it became evident that Julia Thomas had spoken the truth, as had Rinehart Petrasch. And accusations against Petrasch were apparently false.

Jacob Waltz is believed to have told Julia Thomas and Rhinehart Petrasch how to find the mine, and had described two different routes by which they could locate it. But two things must be remembered. First, the desert in the area of the mine is incredibly rough terrain. A person could be standing within five feet of a mine and not see it as such. Second, the sense of proportion in distance is hard to communicate, even on a map. Without accurate measurement and mapping methods, it would be nearly impossible to construct an accurate map. Waltz must have known this from his many years of chasing gold all over the West. And he must have known that no matter what he told them, they'd never find it. But nonetheless, he told them. And he used landmarks which anyone could recognize, if, of course, they went near enough to see them.

So Julia Thomas and Rhinehart Petrasch had probably been correct in their understanding of the Dutchman in spite of accusations of their having been drunk at the time of Waltz's descriptions. Tragically, the interpretation of Weaver's Needle incapacitated them in their search and quest for the mine. They had allowed others to tell them the

Plate 14: Needle Rock at Verde River
(Dutchman's Needle Canyon: Now Camp Creek)

Plate 15: Sombrero Butte in Camp Creek Near Carefree

general location of the Needle (near Apache Junction), and thus the mine, and they never even looked to the north, along the Verde, where the military trail was, where the mine was, at the western end of the Superstition Mountain Range, which it was.

The Dutchman had given many clues, but as Bill, the discoverer knows, the mine was so well hidden by natural terrain that it may never have been found, except by accident.

From the old military trail, Waltz said that he and his partner would camp overnight in the old Spanish rock ranch house. At the start of the trail, there was a shelving rock on the north side (easily seen today). This was the place now referred to as Needle Rock, the concourse of Camp Creek and the Verde River (Plate 14, page 100).

From here he would go up to first water. Waltz described the trail as being a steep, narrow canyon, full of potholes, a well worn trail, that tended in a north-south direction to First Water (a spring where a cottonwood tree grows in Camp Creek), then to Sombrero Butte (Plate 15, page 101). On up to Horse Rock (Plate 11, page 93), to five mile water (Camp Creek above Bartlette Dam Road flows year round for a distance of approximately five miles to a waterfall which usually marks the lower end of the flowing water). When he left the military trail, he came to the Man in the Bushes rock formation (not pictured but easily found), from there to the Saddle (not pictured but easily found), and on up to the round Circle of Rocks (Plate 4, page 15). The Circle of Rocks is a ruin which can be found off Seven Springs Road. From here you could see Four Peaks and Weaver's Needle; they look like one mountain range. There was a large rock formation in the shape of a man's head that looked below on a mine hidden in the bushes. This is the key: From here you go on up to the old workings. While looking from the mine, if you go down ridge and you come to three red hills, you've gone too far. He said the mine was at the western end of the Superstition Mountain range, and north of Weaver's Needle at four o'clock.

The trail that he apparently gave Julia Thomas, because she knew very little about the mountains, he told her from his home on the Salt River in Phoenix. He told her to take the Salt River until she came to the trail and go north. He gave her a trail in from the south. It was the old Pima Trail. From the river, you take the trail and go to Sombrero Mountain (Plate 16, page 104). There was a large sombrero on the mountain. That is now called the McDowell Mountains (easily seen from Pima Road). From here you go to the Eye of the Needle (Plate 12, page 96). The mine lies to the North of the Eye of the Needle. The Eye of the Needle is Pinnacle Peak, and you can clearly see the needle and the eye from Pinnacle Peak Road between Pima Road and Reata Pass. From the Eye of the Needle, thence to Blacktop Hill (not pictured but easily found near Pinnacle

Plate 16: Sombrero Mountain from Pima Road
(Now the McDowell Mountains)

Peak), thence to Blacktop Mesa (Plate 13, page 97), to where the old cow house was (old corrals not pictured but still there). From here you go on over the mountain, down to the big spring. From here, she was to either go down around over the old trails to the base of Sombrero Butte, or to take the trail more to the north, over the little pass there, and down to the big spring (five mile water). Whichever way she went, she would have seen Horse Rock, but if she went the northern route, she wouldn't have seen Sombrero Butte. Now, he said, the mine lies at the head of the gulch. It's on a butte, on the northern slope. It went down on an eighteen inch vein. "As I come up out of the mine, there is a high pinnacle of rock on one hand, and a fortress on the other." There are two mines from which you can see the fortress and the high pinnacle of rock.

The Dutchman's words have survived. "At the bottom of the mine, there is an incomplete tunnel started by the Mexicans. Opposite the tunnel, is the remains of the stone cabin. Up on the side of the hill, there is an incline and a shaft. Up on the top, there is an open pit mine. From the top of the hill, you can see the military trail all the way into Fort McDowell. But you can't see the mine from the military trail. On the hillside below, there is a tunnel, or shaft, on the canyon wall, the mine is on a canyon wall. There are a few red outcroppings around the mine area. Below the mine are three cedar trees and a spring. One of the limbs is sawn off and points to the mine. Directly across from the mine, about a mile and a half, is a cave with a two room cabin. This mine faces the west, the afternoon sun shines directly into the mine when the mine is open. It is at the head of two washes. From the top of the cave, you can see the military trail. But from the military trail, you can't see the cave. From here, you proceed on down canyon, carefully observing the canyon wall. High on a ridge, is a large rock formation in the shape of a man's head, that looks down on a mine hidden in the bushes below. this mine faces the north, it's at the base of a high bluff."

"From the mouth of the mine, looking southward, you can see Weaver's Needle." Picacho Butte, Sombrero Butte, Sombrero Mountain, and the Needle's Eye, were all to the south. Black Top Mountain is to the north of the Large Rock Formation in the Shape of a Man's Head.

Chapter 8

The Dutchman's Trail

I'll just tell you the story, what he told. Waltz gave these clues to Julia Thomas and Rhinehart Petrasch. He said, at the start of the trail there was an old, rock, Spanish house where he and his partner would camp overnight on the way to the mine. He also called this area, Apache Camp. The Indians were known to camp all along the Verde River. It was a day's journey by horse to this spot from his homestead in Phoenix. This was the summer route because there was water all the way.

At the start of the trail, there was a shelving rock on the north side. This also was an eye that you could see the needle [Today this place is called Needle Rock]. Waltz called this canyon Needle Canyon for more than one reason. On the way back from the mine, looking southward for a distance of two to three miles in the canyon, you could see Weaver's Needle. He also said, it was a steep, narrow canyon; it was a well worn trail, full of potholes, that tended in a north-south direction. Then you come to first water.

Then you come to Sombrero Butte. The Mexicans called this the "stone hat." Then to Horse Rock [The Man on the Horse]. From Horse Rock to five mile water, on up to the mouth of the canyon. There was an old stone house at the mouth of the canyon that tended in a north-south direction.

On up the ridge, high on this ridge, there is a large rock formation in the shape of a man's head that looks down on a mine hidden in the bushes below [The first Natural Face]. The second Natural Face looked up to the mine [Dutchman's Mine]. Waltz said, this is the key, when you come to the rock formation in the shape of a man's head, from here you go on up to the old workings. You take the right of two canyons. The mine lies at the head of two washes. From the top of my cave you can see the old military trail. But from the old military trail, you cannot see my cave. This cave has two rooms and faces the west. The afternoon sun shines directly into the mouth of the cave when the mine is open.

About two hundred feet across from the cave, on the north side, is an incline shaft that also faces the west. On the hillside below is a tunnel that was started by Don Miguel Peralta II's father [Don Miguel Peralta]. Across from the mine about a mile and a half, was the second mine. It is on a butte. At the bottom of the butte there is an incomplete tunnel started by the Mexicans. Opposite this tunnel is the remains of a stone cabin. About two hundred feet across from the cave is a shaft. Up on the side of the mountain is a shaft, and up on the top is an open pit mine. The mine is also high on the wall of the canyon. Looking southward from the mouth of the mine you can see Weaver's Needle at four o'clock.

Waltz said, across the ravine, facing the east, is a large rock formation in the shape of a man's head that looks on a mine hidden in the bushes below. There is a spring in the wash by the three pine trees that is sufficient for household use.

He also had a mine high on the side of the mountain. As you come up out of the mine, there is a high pinnacle of rock on one hand, and a fortress on the other.

Julia Thomas knew very little about the mountains, so he gave her a trail from the south. He told her, from Phoenix, to take the Salt River to the trail which went to the north [This trail is now known as Pima Road]. First, you come to Sombrero Mountain [McDowell Mountains], then to the Eye of the Needle [Pinnacle Peak], then to Blacktop Hill [next to Pinnacle Peak], then to Blacktop Mesa [also near Pinnacle Peak], then to the old cowhouse [pens are still there], then on over the mountain to the rock horse [Camp Creek], and to the big springs [Upper Camp Creek where the water runs year round].

Then he said, when he left the military trail [Camp

Creek], go up to the Man in the Bushes that looks to the east. Then on up to the Saddle, and then on up to the round Indian Circle of Rocks [existing ruins]. From the Circle of Rocks, you can't get down there to the bottom of the canyon because it's too steep. Remember, he said she could go all the way on horseback, and the sides to the Circle of Rocks butte are definitely too steep for horseback. Go on back down to the mouth of the canyon, and then on up to the mine.

He also told her, if you go down ridge and come to the three red hills, you've gone too far. Turn around and go back [these are down Camp Creek near Blue Mountain].

Chapter 9

The Lands Between Carefree and Horseshoe Lake

After the death of the Dutchman, there was a frenzy of maps, searches and stories about the lost mine. And other lost mine stories poured into the Valley as well. The Superstition Mountains near Apache Junction had become a magnet for the flocks of Dutchman mine seekers, many of them armed with maps purchased from Julia Thomas. The mysterious mountains also became a magnet for the other lost mine stories. Nearly every lost mine story was wrongly attributed to the vicinity of Weaver's Needle. And the most unlikely hills, buttes, ridges and rocks were believed to be the famed landmarks so often mentioned in all the stories.

One very misleading landmark is Sombrero Mountain. Now that we have accepted the name of the McDowell Mountains for this particular area, it has occured to no one to look for the sombrero which rests so clearly and serenely on the top. But it can be seen clearly from the intersection of Pima Road and Bell Road (in the great Arizona propensity for renaming everything, Bell Road has been recently renamed after Frank Lloyd Wright just as nearly everything in Apache Junction has been named after the Dutchman).

And how many people have driven past Pinnacle Peak and never looked to see the Eye of the Needle? Thousands of ATC's flood Camp Creek every week, scuffing and tearing their way over every possible little scrub of a hill or trail, and yet no one has ever noticed Sombrero Butte. Why? Because people don't look. Just like the discovery of gold at Sutter's Mill, nobody looked *there* for gold. Nobody looked in Camp Creek for Sombrero Butte, either. But they will now. And they will see it, too. It is splendid. And there are many mines yet to be discovered on the basis of the newly located landmarks.

I had a copy of the designs and mappings from Petroglyph Rock in the Superstition Mountains in my hand and as I stood across from the Apache Thunder God, I saw that the drawing on the petroglyph was identical to the stone image in front of me. As the map indicated, and with some help from other text I'd studied, I went across the ravine and up the other side of the hill. As I walked up the other side, I moved to a position where a smaller rock in the distance began to approach the headshaped stone. I continued climbing and moving about until the other rock moved into precisely the position that I could see it occupied on the drawing. The smaller rock even had the same shape as the one cut onto the petroglyph.

When the smaller rock lined up with the stone head, as if to produce the appearance of an ear or backpack, I looked at my feet. There, at my feet, lay the sunken hole of the old Spanish mine! I'd found it.

There are many maps describing lost mines, and many of them are true. Unfortunately, most of the ones published in popular books are not true reproductions, so about all the adventurous searcher can do is find the landmarks because the relationship between the landmarks and the mine location has often been altered to protect the interest of the holder of the map. This is not the case with the stone tablets on display at the Mesa Southwest Museum. These can be viewed directly by anyone (at certain times, at other times they display replicas). The plates in this book are photographs of the real ones.

There have been so many who have searched for the Dutchman Mine, and there have been so many who have searched for the Jesuit and Peralta mines that it boggles the imagination. For approximately one hundred years men have searched and retold the stories. Their imaginations fired, they have spent years of their lives, and some have lost their lives, pondering the riddles and stories, pouring into the desert, in hopes of discovering the magical link to the mines. The clue to the language. The vision of a landmark. The correct perspective.

Now, the landmarks revealed, these adventures can begin again. There must be hundreds of mines which remain to be found. And the value of the other stories of lost mines will increase, now that the correct area can be searched.

The map on the next two pages identifies both the Lost Dutchman Mine and the Circle of Rocks as they appear on the stone tablet pictured in Plate 3, page 14. A transparency of the "heart" enlarged to proper proportions will fit the contours of a modern map, which also shows the shape of a heart in the same area.

All of the mines and symbols for the stone tablets have not yet been interpreted, but there is strong evidence that the tablets pertain to the same general area of Camp Creek and the Lost Dutchman Mine. The full translation of the stone tablets should be realized in the near future, and is, yet, another story.

It is wholeheartedly hoped that each adventurer will remember two things: One, to follow the heart. And two, that the trails are dangerous.

Map of Dutchman's Landmarks. On Plate 3, Page 14, the Circle of Rocks Appears as " ⊙ " in the Center of the Heart.

On Plate 3, Page 14, The Dutchman's Mine is "X" inside the Heart.

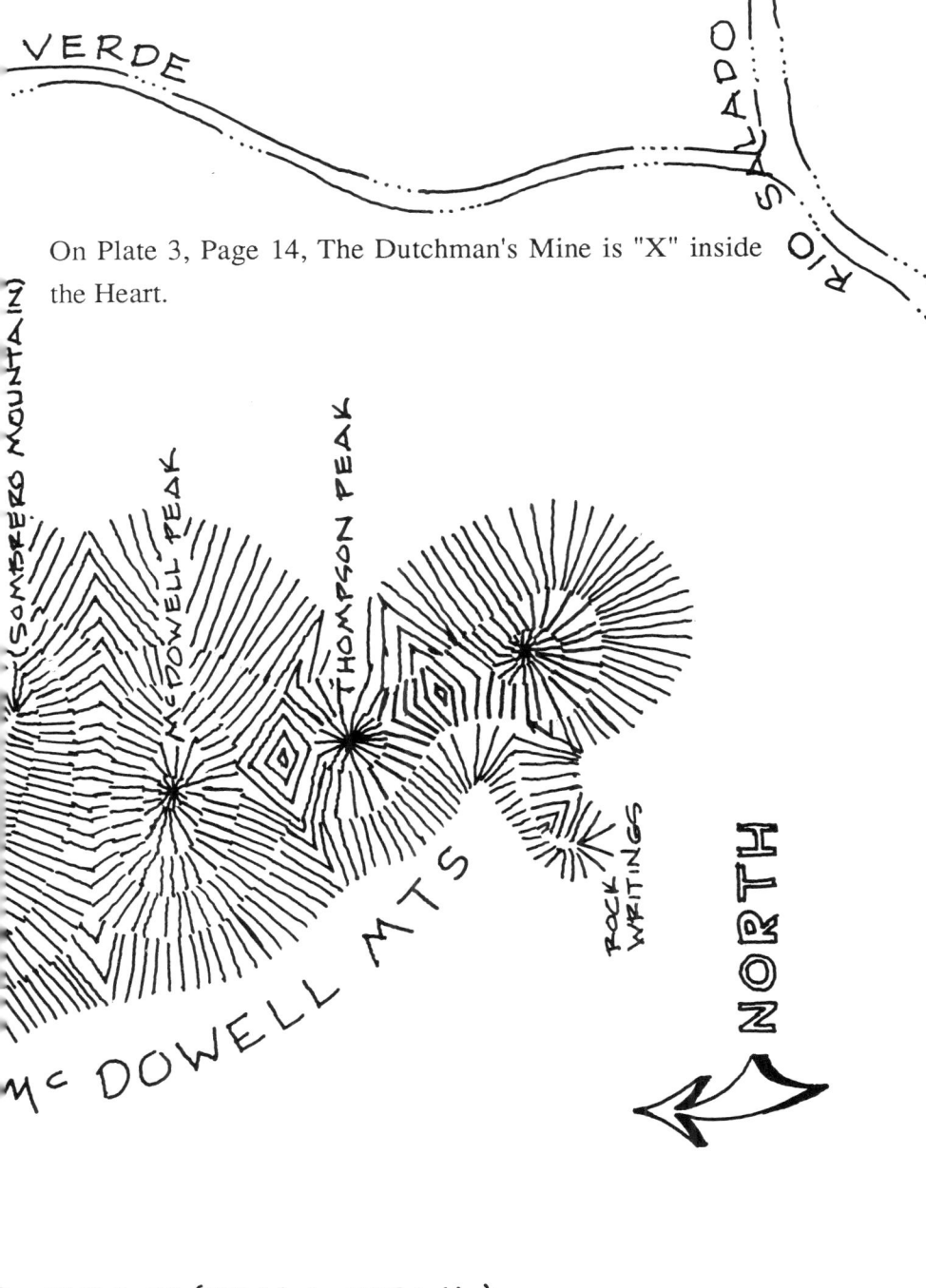

AUTHOR'S NOTE

There are many things which deserve respect in the desert. Artifacts and landmarks are precious and protected by law. Indian ruins are not to be disturbed.

Mining claims are property, and are to be respected. It is unlawful to prospect, mine, or remove rocks or samples from any existing claim, and most claimants will protect their rights therein. It is wise to pay attention to mining monuments and avoid the possibility of trespass.

Many true locations have been revealed in this story, and with the hope that readers will enjoy whatever discoveries await their efforts. All persons engaging in exploration, prospecting and mining activity on public lands are exercising a basic American right, and hopefully, will do so in the spirit appropriate for a free and responsible public.

The Bureau of Land Management in Phoenix maintains a public room for inquiries and claim filing information. Their staff is very knowledgeable and helpful for first time claimants. The State of Arizona also publishes information periodically on how to file and work a claim in Arizona. It has been the experience of this writer that most independent miners are very respectful of the environment, although certain governmental agencies use environmental issues to harrass them and drive them off their claims. It is the responsibility of the public to learn the laws and keep these bureaucrats operating within their true powers.

It was the spirit of mining on a small scale which earned the lands which this book describes, and U.S. citizens still hold the right by law to file claims and work them. It is important that we preserve the spirit of our laws, and the spirit of our people, and the right to follow our own hearts.

ACKNOWLEDGEMENTS

William Scovel, Gary Weesner, Christopher O'Donnell, The Flagg Foundation, Mesa Southwest Museum, Randy Galloway, Ron Clark, Tru Colour, Inc., Kelley Sands, Gary & Terry Kuhstoss, Bernadine, Lorri, Chris Burawa, Charles Boardman, Gordon Whyte, Mike Whyte and Friends, Larry Prall, Doug Speed, Johnny Dust, Frank Maguire and the Staff of the Mill Avenue Merchant's Association.